PAST TIMES

Obituaries, Marriages and Other Selected Articles from the

𝔐𝔞𝔯𝔶𝔳𝔦𝔩𝔩𝔢 𝔗𝔦𝔪𝔢𝔰

Maryville, Tennessee

1884-1890

Caleb Glenn Teffeteller

HERITAGE BOOKS
2008

HERITAGE BOOKS

AN IMPRINT OF HERITAGE BOOKS, INC.

Books, CDs, and more—Worldwide

For our listing of thousands of titles see our website
at
www.HeritageBooks.com

Published 2008 by
HERITAGE BOOKS, INC.
Publishing Division
100 Railroad Ave. #104
Westminster, Maryland 21157

International Standard Book Numbers
Paperbound: 978-0-7884-4580-4
Clothbound: 978-0-7884-7689-1

**This book is dedicated to
my cousin and friend,
Edna McDonell Morris**

Table of Contents

Inroduction

This volume contains obituaries, resolutions of respect, marriage notices and other articles from Blount and surrounding counties. Every effort was made to include each obituary and marriage notice located in existing copies of the *Maryville Times* covering the years 1884 through 1890. Some of the microfilm was hard to decipher and some issues were partially missing or missing altogether. Because an obituary or marriage notice is not given here does not mean there wasn't one. The original copy of the newspaper may have included it but has been torn away or lost since the newspaper's publication and the time it was microfilmed.

Given names and surnames were added in brackets when learned from a reliable source. Some articles including personal letters and court proceedings were not transcribed in full but given reference to so one can read them in their entirety by finding them on the microfilm.

The information contained within was transcribed from one roll of microfilm. Roll # 202 of the *Maryville Times,* 1884-1891, was obtained from the Tennessee State Library and Archives, 403 Seventh Avenue North, Nashville, TN, 37243. This microfilm can also be found and viewed at the Blount County Public Library, 508 N. Cusick, Maryville, TN 37801.

I have enjoyed compiling this information and I hope that it contributes something extra to the family history of others. I transcribed this information the best I could and any errors I hope will be overlooked. This work is in no way meant to be disrespectful to anyone, living or deceased.

Many thanks to the Blount County Public Library, Albert W. Dockter, Martin L. Qualls, and a special thanks to the late Jane Kizer Thomas who referred me to Heritage Books, Inc.

Caleb Glenn Teffeteller
P.O. Box 5413
Maryville, TN 37802

MARYVILLE TIMES

Saturday, October 11, 1884

FAIR!---Yesterday closed the annual exhibition of the Blount County Fair. In the aggregate the fair was a success. About 900 people were on the grounds in the forenoon, and the crowd grew larger toward the time of racing at 4 P.M. The morning was occupied by sweepstakes and an address of Col. **Yearwood**, of Sweetwater. We noticed at the fair grounds a flock of fine Spanish merino sheep that deserves especial mention. It is perhaps the only flock of thoroughbred merinos in this part of the State. We are informed by Prof. **Cate**, the exhibitor, that he sheared fifty-seven pounds of wool from five head which he sold at 50 cents per pound. His Vermont buck, "Colonel," doubtless the finest sheep ever brought into this State. His third fleece weighed twenty-six pounds. A year old buck, "Major," sheared last spring eleven pounds, a ewe lamb of the same age sheared nine pounds. This is certainly a sheep country naturally, and there certainly would be money in keeping good sheep. We would be glad to see farmers raising more sheep and fewer dogs. There is a sure profit in the former if rightly kept and then cared for, while the most of the latter are worse than useless. We hope our next Legislature will give us a good dog law.

A scrub race was made up at the fair grounds yesterday morning which came near proving fatal to Joe **Rhea**. While running his horse, it threw off, landing him against a post. Prompt medical aid soon straightened him out, but he still has some recollection of an earthquake.

The races yesterday were three in number. The only one of interest was the running race, which consisted of four competitors. There was some fast stock on the ground, but for want of competition their speed was not brought out. The following is a summary of yesterday's speed:

Single foot race, two best in three; first money, John **Conner**; second money, Pat **Rasor**.

Trotting race, first money, C.T. **Johnson**; second money, D.L. **King**.

Running race, first money, John **Conner**; second money, Bob **Matthews**.

Tony **Thompson**, the little colored rider, takes the cake. He won the admiration of all present.

FIRE!---Yesterday we received the report of a destructive fire in the 14th District. The burning occurred on the farm of 'Squire John **Gamble**. The steam thresher of **Wilson** and **Everett** had been employed, and on

1

Thursday threshed 16 bushels of clover hay seed; night came and the hands repaired to headquarters to pass the slumber hours. At three o'clock yesterday morning one of the hands went to the thresher to arrange the machinery for operations, and discovered the thresher on fire and the surrounding ground burned black. The fire could not be extinguished, and all was lost. The ten bushels of seed and five loads of hay shared the same fate as the thresher. The losses will amount to over $500. It is not known how the fire originated. They had threshed this season 350 bushels of clover seed, and were promised as much more. The latter is clear loss.

Thursday, January 8, 1885

Ellejoy---Our friend, J.N. **Walker**, who was so badly torn up in the mill, is improving slowly. It is hoped that he will recover. / In olden times there was a prodigal son who left his father and wandered into a far country. He returned and was welcomed. A fattened calf was killed, and there was dancing and making merry. So our friend, H.J. **Jeffries**, returned from Iowa a few days ago, but no calf was killed at this end of the line. The girls may look out for him, for he came back as single as he went.

From Indiana---I received on Christmas Day a copy of your valuable paper, the *Maryville Times*, for Dec. 18. I consider it a very valuable Christmas gift, for which please accept thanks. Through the politeness of George **Neff** I received a copy of the *Times* some time ago. I am always glad to get such favors, especially when they come from Tennessee, the land of my birth. My parents were born and raised in Knox County, Tennessee, and resided there until I was in my third year, when they migrated to Indiana. I have always had a great desire to go and see my native land, and that desire becomes greater each year as people from the North go there and send back such favorable reports.

I have listened to my parents tell of the fine climate, good water and splendid fruits that they used to enjoy in Tennessee. Quite a number of my relations still live in Knox and adjoining counties.

We have had a very nice fall in this county, but for the last three weeks we have had winter. Snow from 10 to 15 inches deep, and the mercury ranging from zero down to 16 below.

Health generally good.

Crops were better this year than for the last three or four years.

Prices of all kinds of farm products have depreciated so much that times are very hard.

2

With many thanks for your kindness,
I am respectfully yours, John C. **Chumlea**, Warren County, Ind.,
Dec. 27, 1884.
The gentleman who writes the above is a cousin of W.C. **Chumlea**,
Clerk of Circuit Court. Though near relatives, time and distance had
made them entire strangers. Luckily, through the medium of the *Times*,
an old and distinguished family is able to re-unite their lost members and
exchange the experience of years.

ON THE WING---Through the kindness of your editors I give you a
brief description of my trip West, also a general description of the
country.
Left Maryville 1st day of March, 1884; bought tickets at Knoxville to
San Francisco---3rd class, $62.90. Left Knoxville 2:40 P.M., and arrived
at Memphis next day at 12 P.M. West of Memphis not much could be
seen but a flood of water and tops of trees. Took the steamer at 5 P.M.,
went about 80 miles down the Mississippi and about 80 miles up the St.
Florence River to Madison which is only 40 miles from Memphis by
R.R.---almost entire track being covered with water. Took the train at 9
A.M., passed through Little Rock, arrived at Texarkana 7:15 P.M.
Saturday the 3rd. Left Texarkana 9 A.M. on the 4th. Split the big state in
two the long way---868 miles by the schedule. Arrived at El Paso 4 A.M.
on the 6th. Southwestern Texas presents a very dry appearance and is
unsettled. Animal curiosities, antelope and prairie dogs. Near Colorado
City, Texas, we narrowly escaped a serious accident. Passing an
unlocked side-switch, the switch become misplaced, let the two hinder-
most cars off and turned them upon their sides. The two overturned cars
contained about 25 persons, some women and children. Our car did not
run off. At El Paso we saw the first adobe houses. These are made of
earth and straw, or grass worked into a mortar and cut as bricks and sun-
dried. Of these are made walls, roofs and all---don't need to turn much
rain. Often saw them through New Mexico and Arizona. Since the
completion of the R.R. many neat villages have sprung up all along the
line from El Paso to Frisco, prominent among which are Deming in New
Mexico, Benson and Tucson in Arizona and many others in California.
Los Angeles is a beautiful city of about 20,000 inhabitants, about 17
miles from the Pacific Ocean. Here, the 8th day of March, were oranges
on the trees, some ripe and some green and blossoms for new ones.
Between Los Angeles and Frisco is some fine country; but along the R.R.
its greater part is dry and mountainous, in many places irrigation is
necessary to successful farming. Reached San Francisco on the 11th at 10
A.M. Of course it wouldn't be expected that I describe a city; but suffice

to say it is a big one, about 250,000 inhabitants; stayed there three days, visited the Cliff House on the seashore. It presented a grand view of the ocean and a large cliff several hundred feet from the shore. Hundreds of sea lions were climbing these rocks and tumbling off into the water, and continuously putting up their pitiful howl. Many other attractions too tedious to mention. Bought tickets to Portland, second class $10.00, boarded the steam ship Wednesday 14th, at 10 A.M., and soon was out of sight of land. In short, was sick, sicker, sickest, and for 36 hours was very sick. On the ocean three days and two nights. In the mouth of the Columbia River is a sand bar which can be crossed with safety only during high tide. We floated outside the bar about an hour and a half waiting for the tide. On the bar could be seen part of the Great Republic which was wrecked in 1878; think John A. **McReynolds** went out on this ship only a few trips before it was wrecked. We crossed the bar just at sun down; stopped at Astoria, then pulled out for Portland at 4 o'clock, A.M., the 17th; didn't see much of the city, but it ranks prominent among the leading commercial cities in the United States. Bought tickets to Walla Walla, Washington for $13.60. No reduced rates on these roads. Reached Walla Walla about 9:30 P.M. on the 17th.
---Respectfully, H.T. **Clemens**, Pampa, Whitman Co. Washington Territory.

MARRIED---Dec. 18, at the residence of the bride's father, in Akron, Harrison Co. Mo., by the Rev. D.W. **Reur**, the Rev. Charles C. **Hembree** and Miss. Rosa **Frazier**.
Mr. Hembree is a graduate of Maryville College, class '77, and is well known throughout East Tennessee.

Miss. Ella H. **Evans**, dress-maker, late of Tuscola, Ill., now located with Mrs. L.E. **Smith**, Maryville, is prepared to do all kinds of work in the dress-making line at reasonable rates. Cutting and fitting and patterns a specialty at following rates: Basques, .50 cts; Basque and Sleeve pattern, .25 cts; Over dress, Suits cut and planned ready to make, $1.50. Miss. Evans brings latest designs for all kinds of suits, and with her long experience guarantees satisfaction to all.

Brick Mill, December 29--- Christmas is over. We had a Christmas tree at Woods' School House and would have had a good time but whiskey controlled a portion of the crowd, and you can judge the conduct of the crowd. I think it was the most ill-behaved crowd I have met since the war. Robert **Armstrong**, an aged citizen of this community, died last Thursday night. The wife of Samuel **McCammon** died on last Friday.

4

J.B. **Lane** and wife are rejoicing in the birth of two fine boys; weight 10 and 10 ½ pounds.

Sumner S. **Kirk**, of whose death we gave notice last week, died of typhoid fever; his illness lasted three days. He was buried in Washington City; he was about 30 years old.

Miss. Birdie **Smith**, daughter of Mrs. L.E. Smith, met with a serious accident on Monday. While watching a game of ball among her school mates she was struck across the forehead with a ball bat. Dr. **Arbeely** dressed the wound.

The many friends of Mr. William **Burton** will be grieved to learn of his demise, which occurred last Thursday at his residence near, Ebenezer, Knox County. Mr. Burton was a resident of this county for many years, and was the father of Mr. William Burton of this place.

Mr. G.A. **Howe** and family, Vicksburg, Miss., have located in our community and will make Maryville their future home. Mr. Howe comes in our midst highly recommended as a gentleman, worthy of our respect. It stands our citizens in hand to extend a cordial hand to them and make them feel that they are one of us.

The two horses of Dr. **Stanley** were left standing in front of a furniture store Monday, hitched to a wagon, containing a partial load of new furniture. Making the best of the good opportunity, the horses started east on Main Street with the wagon and furniture following at break-neck speed. The furniture was disturbed along the road for some distance, and a pair of the wagon wheels were tossed gently to the sidewalk at different intervals, but the horses stopped not to gather up the fragments.

Quite a social event occurred at the residence of Mr. & Mrs. George **Kizer**, Rockford, last Wednesday the 31st ult. It was the marriage of Mr. William **Russell**, of Knox Co., to Miss. Nellie **Wright**, youngest daughter of late D.S. and N.J. **Wright**, in the presence of the immediate friends of the contracting parties. The ceremony was performed at 3 o'clock P.M. in a very impressive manner by the Rev. Donald **McDonald** of this place. The attendants were: Mr. Charles T. **Cates**, Jr., and Miss. Jennie **Kizer**; Mr. Charles **Badgett** and Miss. Ida **Walker**. After the bride and groom had received many congratulations, all were invited to the spacious dining hall, where they enjoyed a sumptuous dinner. The presents were many and costly.

At night the "light fantastic toe" was tripped to the sweet strains of music, and when the sun had run more than half his successive midnight journey, proud Morpheus smiled upon them and welcomed them to his refreshing, shadowy lands. We extend to Mr. & Mrs. Russell hearty congratulations and best wishes for a life of happiness.

Thursday, July 23, 1885

John E. **Toole**, son of Col, James M. **Toole** and brother to Robert P. **Toole**, of the *Herald*, died at the residence of his father, corner Wood and Preston Streets at 1:30 p.m. yesterday, after a lingering illness of typhoid fever, in the 22nd year of his life. The deceased was a young man of excellent qualities of head and heart and was generally liked by all who knew him. The *Times* extends sympathies to the bereaved family. The funeral will take place from the First Presbyterian Church at 4:30 p.m. The friends and acquaintances of the family are invited to be present. --- *Dallas* (Texas) *Weekly Times*.

The deceased was also a brother to our fellow townsman, George A. **Toole**.

J.M. **Johnston** and lady, of Louisville, lost their only child last week by death.

Walter, son of the late W.D. **McGinley**, died last Thursday at his mother's residence near town.

Two children in the family of Lewis **George** died recently; one died on Saturday night, the other one on Sunday evening.

Mr. El. **Wright**'s wife died on Saturday last, near Mt. Tabor, and was buried the following day in that neighborhood.

Mrs. E.W. **Wright**, of the 10th district, died at her home on Thursday, the 16th. She was the youngest daughter of the late Benjamin **James**. The deceased was a member of Mt. Tabor Presbyterian Church. Aged about 49 years. Rev. E.A. **Elmore** conducted the funeral obsequies.

Hiram **Bogle**, formerly a resident of the county, near Eusebia, died at his farm residence near Nashville on June 10th. Aged about 65.

In last week's issue we made an error in stating that S.E. **Hoyle** had

6

buried a child. It was the child of David **Hoyle** who returned from the west last spring. Its age was five months and fourteen days.

In Memoriam---Died on the 7th inst., at the residence of her brother-in-law, J.P. **Raulston**, Miss. Amanda **Hannah** in the seventy-eighth year of her age. The deceased was the daughter of the late Matthew **Hannah**, and was born and lived on the farm, or in the vicinity of where she died, all her long sojourn here on earth. In early youth and womanhood she is said to have been a woman of remarkable intelligence, and of a kind and amiable disposition. Sometime prior to the year 1830 she professed faith in Christ and united with the New Providence Presbyterian Church and lived a very pious and devoted Christian life, an evidence of which is given by her surviving sister who remembers well the times that she was taken by the deceased to a secluded spot in their father's woodland, where she was in the habit of spending a season in sweet communion with God, and endeavored to impress on her youthful mind the beauty of a life of Godliness. But in the midst of this promising life, a dark pall suddenly spreads over her path, and ere long with sadness her family realizes that the noble reason that made the daughter and sister so attractive, is completely dethroned, and for fifty years or more she was destined to live in a state of aberation of mind, leading her to fancy all manner of frightful disasters as occurring around her, and in which her friends were involved, and from which she apparently believed she was under obligations to relieve them. But strange as it was she never complained of her own troubles but always of that of others, whose fancied condition rendered her miserable. But, at least, her troubles are over, and she is doubtless reaping the reward of her faithfulness while competent to serve the Lord. The funeral exercises were conducted in the Liberty Meeting House on the 8th inst., by Rev. James V. **Iddins**, after which the body was interred in the graveyard adjoining.

> "Ramble the hills where in youth we did stray,
> When I am gone, when I am gone.
> Visit the place where we oft went to pray,
> When I am gone, when I am gone."

J.V.I.

Mrs. Anna B. **Davis**, of Knoxville, who is on her way to the springs, is making a short stay at Mr. **Hanna**'s home. Mrs. Davis was seriously injured in a railway accident at Ashland, Ill., on the L. & N. Railroad in

October 1882. She still suffers from that shock; yesterday she took her second railway ride in three years. Formerly, Mrs. Davis was a great traveler.

On Monday evening, the 13th inst., a strange man came into the post office and spoke to Capt. **Kirk**, but was not recognized by the Captain. Whereupon he made himself known as Alfred A. **Wyatt**, formerly of North Carolina, and during the late unpleasantness was a member of Capt. Kirk's company. He was wounded in the same engagement in which the Captain was shot, but had not seen each other since that day. The Captain was rather incredulous and insisted upon seeing the scar where he was wounded before he would be convinced; whereupon the scar was exhibited which fully satisfied the doubting Thomas, and very hearty greetings were exchanged, and Mr. Wyatt was cordially invited home by the Captain and spent a very pleasant night under his hospitable roof where their old war experiences were fully recounted and lived over again, and the visit proved to be a most enjoyable one all around. Mr. Wyatt's home at present is Knoxville, and he returned Tuesday morning much pleased with his visit.

In Memory Of Little Earnest---Infant son of Cabe and Mary **Best**, age 11 months, departed this life June 17; was sick but a short time. All was done for little Earnest that love could do. But alas, death calls for its own. Funeral services were conducted by Rev. **Taylor**. The remains of the budding rose were laid to rest in Carpenter's Graveyard.

"Young mother and father, he is gone
His dimpled cheek no more will touch thy breast;
No more the music tone
Float from his lips to thine all fondly pressed
His smile and happy laugh are lost to thee;
Earth must his mother and his pillow be."

In Memory Of Little Carrie---Who departed this life, June 15. The deceased was nineteen months of age, was an only child of Tom and Kate **Thompson**. She was a sweet child, with laughing, blue eyes and beautiful golden curls. Carrie was very intelligent and a most obedient child. But alas, the angel of death came this way, and stole the little jewel from our midst. Home now seems silent and lonely without her. We hear no more of the patter of her little feet or the prattle of her tongue. Funeral services was conducted by Rev. J.A. **Ruble**. Her remains were laid to rest in Carpenter's Graveyard.

"Sweet laughing child---the cottage door
Stands free and open now.
But oh, its sunshine gilds no more
The gladness of thy brow.
The merry step hath passed away,
Thy laughing sport is hushed for aye."

James **Lowe** received word Tuesday night from his wife, who is at
Mrs. **Pugh**'s ten miles below town, that his little boy was seriously ill
with the croup. Mrs. Lowe has been there for several days visiting. We
were unable to find out how serious the little fellow was attacked.

Thursday, July 30, 1885

Out West---Editors Times: In my western home I have caught a
glimpse of the *Maryville Times*, and while looking over its contents I
thought I would give you a sketch of our travels west, though it will be a
poor one, for I was only a child when I left my native land.

Bidding a long adieu to my friends and relatives we left our home in
Tennessee on the 18th of October, 1873. We had a dreadful trip on
account of cold weather. We had snow for several days in Kentucky and
Illinois. We rested with one exception on Sundays; then we were on
Cumberland Mountains and could not get provisions. We also stopped
for a few days in Wright County, in the eastern part of Missouri, at John
Hutsell's, an old friend of my father and a native of Tennessee.

We are well pleased with our home, surrounded by prairie on all sides.
We have not the advantage of many springs, but our wells are good, pure
and healthy, and the country beautified beyond description. I could talk
to you for an hour of the lovely prairie, of the beautiful birds and flowers,
but my girlish heart still pines for my former home. I will now close lest
my simple story be consigned to the waste basket.   ----Julia **Raulston**.
Grangeville, Newton Co. Mo. July 16, 1885.

George P. **Rhea** and Mary **Ammons** were married Thursday, the 23
ult., by S.F. **Cowan**, Esq. The contracting parties were sitting in their
buggy in the road when the ceremony was performed.

Riley **Cupp** has purchased the property formerly occupied by **West**'s
near the railroad, and will proceed to renovate and improve it for a family
residence. We congratulate him for more reasons than one.

Ira and George **Whaley**, of Sevier County, were arraigned before Commissioner **McTeer**, Monday charged with illicit distillation of spirits. The evidence of their guilt was strong enough to bind them over to appear in Federal Court.

Hugh **Wheeler**, an inmate of the county jail, made good his escape last Tuesday afternoon while under the supervision of Joseph **Clemens**. They were at work in rear of the jail building. Wheeler, watching his chances, jumped the fence and made over the hill toward Captain **Hannum**'s at a lively rate. A hot pursuit failed to overtake him. The boys returned red hot.

S.B. **Jones**, a deaf mute, colored young man, hailing from the asylum at Raleigh, North Carolina, attracted considerable attention upon Main Street last Thursday. He was on his way home in Kentucky. About 10 a.m. he was attacked with an epileptic spasm in front of John **McCulloch**'s residence, which came very near ending his sojourn on this sphere of physical maladies. Dr. **Blankenship** was summoned and gave the sufferer considerable aid. After he partially recovered he was able to make known his wants, and was cheerfully aided by numerous persons about town. His condition was indeed a lamentable one and a worthy object of charity. Friday morning he was started on his way rejoicing.

An article on the death of Myrtle **Dyer** should have appeared in this column, but by an accident it was omitted.

Thursday, August 13, 1885

A Serious Mistake---On last Saturday, while in attendance upon the Baptist Association at Piney Level Church, Col. A.J. **Neff** was taken ill with symptoms of pneumonia. He was conveyed to his home in Maryville. A number of doses of quinine was administered during Saturday night, and on Sunday, about 1:30 p.m. called for more quinine. His little daughter, Nellie, heard the request and started for the quinine. It had been placed under the clock, on a small bracket, but by some means a package of arsenic had been placed there, and in reaching for the quinine, procured the arsenic. Opening the paper in her hand she took it to her father, from which he took about ten grains. He remarked at the time that it had a peculiar taste, but paid no more attention to the matter until he was taken violently ill and commenced vomiting. The package was then examined and the mistake discovered. Medical aid was at once summoned and an emetic administered. The evil effects were partially counteracted. Considerable suffering has been the result of the mistake. It is to be hoped that the danger is past, but owing to the slowness of the action of arsenic, the result cannot be given.

A child of Daniel **Whitehead**'s died on the 5th inst., with flux.

A child of Cowan **Long**, in the 8th district, died on the 8th inst., with flux.

James **Snyder**, living in the Wallace Neighborhood, died on the evening of the 9th, of fever.

Mrs. Fannie **Mead**, of Louisville, left for New York last Thursday to attend the funeral of her mother.

James **Spears**, whom we mentioned before as being very ill with fever, has taken a relapse, and is now in a bad condition.

Lizzie **Wilson**, daughter of Ned Wilson, died on the 7th inst., and was interred in New Providence burying grounds on the 8th inst.

Died, of heart disease, Mrs. Elizabeth **Farr**, the widow of the late James Farr, at the residence of A.B. **Hanna**, Huffstetler's Store, Aug. 9, 1885. The deceased was about sixty years old. At 12 o'clock Sunday she was apparently as well as ever, but at 3 p.m., the death angel called her home.

At Mrs. Fannie **Mead**'s residence, in Louisville, on the 10th inst., a terrific storm took place, the lightning striking a large tree just in front of the house, tearing it to pieces, destroying the fence, injuring the servant girl, killing chickens and doing other damage about the place.

The thermometer marked 97 on Sunday and Monday.

17th District---A little daughter of Mr. Ben **Large** died on the 4th. Little Adria is now at rest where sickness and trouble are felt and known no more.

Cloyd's Creek---Our community was visited by one of the most terrific storms on the night of the 7th. Mrs. J.R. **Hair** had a smoke house and crib blown away, and M.H. **Cochran**, John **Greer** and J.E. **Klepper** had their corn blown down, besides several fruit trees entirely demolished. Large trees in the forest were uprooted and twisted off, and the roads were obstructed. The cyclone was confined to a narrow strip about one mile wide. It was accompanied by heavy rain and thunder; the lightning was a continuous sheet without any interval. ---J.E.K. August 10, 1885.

For the *Times* On the Death of Ellen **Moore**,
Written by her sorrowing sister, Fannie **Fare:**

"Farewell, dear sister, for awhile,
Rest in thy bed of clay,
Until at last we meet again,
At the great judgment day.

Thou art gone from this low land
Of sorrow, grief, and pain;
Thy spirit's roaming with the blest,
On Eden's sunny plain.

We'll feel quite sad indeed to think,
We can never see thee no more,
But yet we know thou art not lost,
But only gone before.

We'll only wait, God knows how long,
As who can tell how soon,
The dear one we have loved so well,
Is called to meet her doom.

And when upon that judgment day,
The trumpet loud shall sound,
God grant we may for Jesus sake,
On His right hand stand.

She is gone to our home, gone to our God,
She was laid in that cold narrow bed.
Bright are the dew drops that light on
The grass that waves gently o'er her head.

Yet she was laid in that cold narrow bed,
It was her spirit we loved, is the loved
Spirit there, the spirit of love called her

Spirit above redeemed from sin and sorrow."

Thursday, August 20, 1885

Golden Wedding---On Wednesday of last week, February 2, occurred the fiftieth or golden wedding anniversary of the marriage of Green **Farmer** and Jennie **Waters**, which took place in the State of Tennessee in the year 1826. At that time "Uncle Green" was a handsome youth of twenty-one summers, while "Aunt Jenny" was a blushing maid, just "sweet sixteen." What assurance had they at that time that half a century hence they would be standing side by side and renewing the vows they had taken to "love and honor?" For fifty years have this aged couple climbed the hill of life together, have shared the same joys and griefs, borne the same burdens and achieved the same triumphs. Together they have seen generations rise up around them and pass away, and standing today the connecting links, as it were, between the first and last half of a nation's history, the representatives of the early western pioneer, is it any wonder that their friends and relatives should delight in according to them that love and affection which is ever the reward of a well spent and useful life? In 1833 the young couple left Blount County, Tennessee, for the then young but rapidly advancing State of Illinois, and in the following year they settled on the farm on which they now reside. For forty-two years, more than the average life-time of man have their interests been identified with the interests of Washington County, The changes they have witnessed have been manifold and startling. They have seen what was then little more than a wilderness changed to one of the most fertile and wealth-producing sections of our great nation. They have seen towns and villages spring up around them, have witnessed the advent of the railroad and telegraph, and have seen with silent admiration and awe the rapid manner in which old things were made to stand aside and give place to the demands of a more advanced civilization. The occasion of the fiftieth anniversary was celebrated in a very quiet way, none but relatives of the old couple being present. There were no offerings of golden presents, but all sat down to an excellent dinner, prepared under the direction of Aunt Jenny, after which all present engaged in social converse which is ever pleasant to the re-united members of a widely-scattered family. Representatives of every family related to the aged couple were present save one, and before they dispersed Uncle Green distributed fifty dollars in coin to the party, giving to each person present something, while the female heads of the families were each presented with a $5 gold piece. May Uncle Green and Aunt Jenny have many more anniversaries of the day on which they began to "climb the hill together," and when at last they are called to go, may they "sleep together at the foot," is our earnest wish.

Green **Montgomery** and Kittie **McCollum** were married at the bride's home, in Loudon County, on the 12th inst. Rev. M.L. **Sloop**, officiating.

Mr. A.C. **Gilchrist** and daughter are recuperating at Black Sulphur. After remaining there until the warm weather is past, they will remove to California to make their future home.

Saturday morning, Frank **Willard** was driving a horse with a load of lumber down the hill on Central Avenue, when the lumber slipped forward and tickled the horse's leg. The horse not liking this and thinking that if he would run he would get out of the way, proceeded to do so. He ran a couple of hundred yards until the hill on Main Street became too much for him, and he then succumbed to the unremitting efforts of Mr. Willard to stop him.

On last Saturday, William **Hickey** was driving Mr. W.C. **Chumlea**'s fine team of horses home from the picnic at Cave Spring. While crossing the railroad near Mr. James **Goddard**'s residence, some thoughtless boys commenced hollooing. The horses became frightened and ran away. They ran about a hundred yards, and one of them fell and kicked himself under the tongue of the wagon, thereby giving the inmates of the wagon opportunity to get out. The front end of the wagon bed was torn to pieces and the legs of both animals badly skinned, rendering one of them temporarily lame. This, we understand, is the extent of damages.

Col. A.J. **Neff**, senior editor of the *Times*, is recovering slowly from the effects of the poison. He is able to be about the house. Considerable time will be required to repair the injuries, but the attending physician thinks it will not be long before he is able to attend to business.

Obituary---Written in memory if Myrtle **Dyer**, who died on the evening of July 22, 1885, at 9:30 P.M. The deceased was a daughter of Mr. & Mrs. John A. **Dyer**. She had been sick but a few days previous to her death. We were not looking for the cold hand of death to fall upon her when it did, but the ways of God are mysterious, and in the very midst of life we are in death. Alas! The angel of death has visited our home and took our little jewel from our home. Home now seems silent and lonely without her; we can not hear the patter of her little feet, or the prattle of her little tongue. It seems so hard to see her little rocking chair and play things idle. But God knows best and doeth all things well. She was a sweet child, with blue eyes always sparkling, with silken sunny hair. She always wanted to help in everything that was to do, although she was only 4 years, 8 months, 6 days old. She could not bear to leave her ma a few hours without kissing her good-bye. The day she died she told Josie, her little sister, to feed Brit, her little dog.

"Oh! Our darling little sister,
Over your silent grave we look,
While above you and around you,
The birds are singing in every nook.

Sleep, Myrtle, sleep thy toils are over,
Well have we loved you,
But God loved you more,
He called you away to that bright happy shore."

Written by Jo and Ella **Dyer**.

Wednesday, January 6, 1886

From a person who made the count expressly for the purpose of counting, we learn that there were over 300 saddle horses hitched at various points in town Monday. It would seem incredible, but it is, nevertheless, true.

Rev. John F. **Hunt**, of the 11th District, died on the 2nd inst., in the 78th year of his age. His funeral occurred on the 4th inst., by Rev. J.A. **Ruble**. He was engaged for more than forty years an active minister in the Baptist Church and was a member of the same organization for more than 48 years. He was well known and all who knew him esteemed him for his perfect manliness and integrity. Few men of his opportunities have accomplished so much in the great battle of life.

Dr. M.F. **Gourley** and family have removed from their home near Louisville to Montague, Texas. The doctor and family have hosts of friends, who regret to see them leave Blount County. The *Times* can cheerfully recommend them to the community in which they shall settle.

Gravel Branch---Mrs. Jack **Black** died last Wednesday. She was interred at Logan's Chapel.
John **Parkins** buried an infant Christmas Day at Piney Level.

15

Ellejoy---On the night of the 26th inst., Mr. John **Robinson**, of this place, lost his house and all it contained except his family, by fire. They awoke just in time to make their escape.

Wednesday, January 13, 1886

At Rockford, about 6 o'clock last Saturday morning, the large barn belonging to J.H. **Davis** was destroyed by fire. A horse, two mules, 400 bushels of corn, a wagon and a lot of hay and roughness were a total loss. The origin of the fire is not known. Mr. Davis had been at work, with his teams, at the marble quarries at Concord, and had just come home to make preparation for farm work for the coming season. He has the sympathy of all.

On last Saturday morning the Government thermometer at the home of the editor, registered four degrees above zero at 4 o'clock. On each succeeding morning, at the same time and place, the mercury fell, until Monday morning, when it actually got down to four below.
Later---Tuesday morning it went down to 8 below and now we are going to stop. If the thing bursts we shall say nothing about it.

Uncle Alexander **Kennedy** celebrated his 84th birthday, last week, with a good old-fashioned turkey dinner. Quite a number of his intimate friends were invited. The *Times* returns thanks for being remembered and trusts that he may live to enjoy many more such occasions.

Hu **Williams** was brought to Maryville last Friday, by Will **Freshour**, to answer for some misdemeanors committed on Ellejoy. The trial was set for Monday, but owing to the severity of the weather the prosecuting witness was not able to appear and Williams was allowed to go free.

State News---Jonathan **Davis**, who lives east of Rockford, had his barn, horses, mules, grain and hay burned, last week, amounting to about $2,000.

State News---Rev. Mr. **Wilson**, of Mossy Creek, died on the 5th instant. He had reached the ripe age of 87 years.

Wednesday, January 20, 1886

A wild man was captured in a cave in the Chilhowee Mountains and taken to Athens. He is now on exhibition at Chattanooga. At the time he was captured he was very poorly clad, having only a few rags on his body. For twelve years he has lived on chickens and such things as he could get in the woods, having communication with no person.

John **McHenry**, of Wabash, Ind., was in Maryville last Saturday. His ancestors were formerly from Blount County. Mr. McHenry spent Sunday with friends near Ellejoy.

Wednesday, January 27, 1886

Died---At the old homestead in the 13th district of Blount County, Mrs. Elizabeth **Thomas**, on January 20, 1886. Mrs. Thomas was born in Carter Co., this State, in the year 1803. She was married to John Thomas, who survives her, in the year 1821. He maiden name was Elizabeth **Daniel.**
She died as she had lived, a consistent member of the Primitive Baptist Church. She leaves a number of children to benefit by her example. The husband is bereft. Mrs. Thomas' own children number 12; her grandchildren number 75; her great-grandchildren 65. Grandma is dead. Baptist papers please copy.

A Murder Trial---Miller's Cove furnishes a sensational case for Court gossip this week. August 10th, 1883, B.F. **Abbott**, an aged citizen of that neighborhood, died suddenly, which caused some excitement. During the last session of the Grand Jury, a bill charging B.F. Abbott, Jr., with the murder of his father, was filed by David **Settlemyer**, of Cades Cove. The Grand Jury investigated the circumstances and found a true bill. The case is booked for this term, but whether a trial will be reached is not certain. We are not in possession of the full particular and as the matter has been little talked of, we are unable to state whether there is any damaging evidence against the defendant.

Married In Tuckaleechee---Will **Fancher** and Mary J. **McCampbell** were united in the holy bonds of matrimony on last Wednesday at the home of the bride's parents, Mr. & Mrs. Isaac **McCampbell**, in Tuckaleechee Cove. Squire **Wester** performed the ceremony in his usual good natured style. We understand the happy couple were treated to a variety of music the evening after the ceremony. Mr. Fancher's home is at present at Sexton, Indiana, having gone from here about four years ago. After visiting among his old acquaintances for a week or two they will repair to the North for a home.

17

Deceased---The death of Mrs. Julia A., wife of R. Lee **Thompson**, has been briefly mentioned in the *Times*.

She died of consumption, on the 2nd inst., after a lingering illness of several months which she bore with much Christian fortitude and composure. Deceased was the daughter of Joshua **King**, of Knox County, and was born on the 21st day of July, 1847, in Knox County, and she was united in marriage to William **Thompson** on the 25th of May, 1871, by Rev. T.J. **Lamar**.

She was a most exemplary wife and mother and a most excellent woman and highly esteemed in the community in which she lived, but had never united with the Church until a short time previous to her death, when she connected herself with the New Providence Presbyterian Church, although she had given good evidence of conversion some years previous.

Her remains were deposited in Magnolia Cemetery on the 4th, after funeral services conducted by Rev. D. **McDonald**. Deceased leaves a devoted husband and an only son and a large circle of kindred and friends to lament her departure.

An Adventure---I had long contemplated a visit to Blount County and arriving here from Knoxville on Friday evening the 16th of January, my object was to find the whereabouts of an Uncle Thomas **McHenry**, with whom I had eaten dinner at my father's home in Rockbridge County about 50 years ago. At Knoxville I met General **Hood**, who directed me to his mother, Mrs. E.A. Hood, for information as to my McHenry kin. I took a hack Saturday morning and, following her directions, I found a friend in the person of Col. James **Davis**, seven miles out on Little River, who directed me to the only surviving heir of my Uncle Tom. The ice was running high, but one of the Colonel's natives landed me safe across by the use of a dug-out. A Mr. **Headrick** kindly furnished me a horse and mule, and his son to pilot me, and I arrived safe at my widow cousin's (wife of Samuel **McHenry**, deceased). I was kindly cared for and the next day took a pair of mules, in company with a driver and three of the family, and drove twelve miles to the Andrew **Rogers** farm, and to the house of one **Latham**, where I found the only surviving daughter of Thomas McHenry. After my many sad inquiries as to the different relatives, including two aunts, Mrs. **Hafley** and Mrs. **McMurrey**, and uncle Thomas, I returned safely and re-crossed the Little River. I spent the night at Col. Davis', who kindly entertained me and brought me to Maryville. It reminded me of the Scripture language: "Beloved, thou doest faithfully what thou doest to the Brethren and to Strangers."

I received, through the kindness of my cousin, several letters from my Uncle John to Thomas, written in Rockbridge County, Va., and dated as far back as 1817; and one from my father, Edward **McHenry**, to his brother Thomas, dated 1818. These letters have the old style seal and twenty-five cents postage.

I had a rough trip but was much pleased with the people and country and shall return again. ---John A. **McHenry**.

The new street, called **Henry** Avenue, is to be opened out from the crossing of Pistol Creek, at Walker's Mill, east to East Street, not far from the south side of the Hackney Mill property. There are some fine situations on that street.

James **Headrick**, infant son of D.R. **Headrick**, died on the 20th.

Solomon **Farmer**, an aged citizen of the 14th district, died on the 18th inst., and was buried on the 19th. Mr. Farmer was nearly eighty years old and stood very highly by all who knew him.

College Notes---We are sorry indeed to hear of the murder committed in Huntsville, one week ago, of Mr. **Pemberton**, who was shot by Mr. **Johnson**. Mr. Pemberton was a student of Prof. David **Clemens** and lady, class '85. We do not know the particulars.

Friendsville---Sylvester **Potter**'s father was buried here yesterday; Sexton Bros. furnished the coffin.

Carpenter's Campground---Mr. Henry **Gourley**, an aged citizen of Happy Valley, died on the 15th inst., of consumption; he was a member of the Baptist church.

Seaton---At a candy treat at Matt. **Williams** the other night some household furniture was demolished by the participants; shame, boys and girls, the next time you go try and tear the house down. Little Laura **Bird** has caught a martin; she says she is going to pet it. I think that if it comes another such a cold spell it will freeze if she don't keep it close. Her mamma wants her to let it go, but she says if it dies it will die hers. There has been two deaths in our midst within the last few weeks. John **Everett**, an aged citizen, died at the residence of his son, James, on the 29th ult., and was interred the next day in the Piney Level burying grounds. On the 3rd inst., an infant of Mr. & Mrs. Andrew **Nuchols**.

19

Along Nine Mile---Mercury down to 13 below zero. Nine Mile was blocked with ice for several days. Plenty of ice in Tennessee River two feet thick. Lots of birds and small animals frozen to death. Coldest weather ever known at this point. / Died, on the 8th inst., Palmer **Brannum**, an aged man. Death resulted from the effects of a broken limb. / Died, on the 9th inst., an infant of Samuel **Howard**, aged days; and on the 10th an infant son of Dr. **Robbins**, found dead in bed; cause of death not known. / Died, on the 12th inst., Mary E. **Bett**, of consumption, aged about 26 years; she was resigned to her fate and ready to die.

Wednesday, February 3, 1886

Mrs. Mary **Tulloch**, of this county, has received a pension by the death of her son in the late rebellion. The sum was $1929.65

The family and household goods of William **Colbert** have arrived from Indiana. They will occupy the house formerly occupied by N.H. **Badgett**.

In the obituary notice of Mrs. Julia **Thompson** last week we made a mistake in stating she was united in marriage to William Thompson. It should have read R. Lee **Thompson**.

D.A. **Lowe** left Maryville last Wednesday morning for Brenham, Texas, to reside in the future. Mr. Lowe has a brother at the same place, who is engaged in the lumber business.

Drs. **Williamson**, **Jones** and **Anderson**, recently performed a surgical operation on Thomas **Logan**, who lives near Big Spring. Mr. Logan was afflicted with a double hair lip, and at last account he was doing very well.

Alfred H. **Keeble** and Rachel F. **Donaldson**, of the 11th district, were married at the residence of James Donaldson, the bride's father. Rev. J.H. **Coulter** was present to pronounce them one. The whole affair was kept a secret until the ceremony was over.

Samuel **Malcom**, Postmaster at Eusebia, brought us in an old hymn book published December 1st, 1718, which makes it 168 years old. It was the property of Grandfather William **Malcom**, who once lived near Eusebia Presbyterian Church, of which he was an Elder.

Mr. Decatur **Bidwell**, who resided in Maryville some months since, but who returned to his former home in Dakota, at Eagen, died on the 20th of January. Mr. Bidwell was a sufferer for years. He visited California and then came to Eastern Tennessee, but the climate of neither locality had the desired effect.

Mrs. Mary **Wilson**, the wife of Oscar Wilson, died at 8 o'clock Monday evening. The funeral services were held this morning at the 2nd Presbyterian Church, Prof. **Crawford** conducting the exercises. A husband and seven children are left to mourn the loss of an affectionate wife and mother.

Married, at the residence of J. Landon **Wallace**, Mr. William **Belt** and Miss Hester A. **Dailey**, Rev. J.V. **Iddins** officiating. After the wedding was over Mr. Wallace took the chair and appointed Richard **Yearout** and Miss Bettie **Wear** a committee to arrange a time and place for the next wedding. It is understood now that matters are progressing nicely in that direction and the editors are desirous of hearing of the occasion in time to enjoy the feast themselves.

Wednesday, February 10, 1886

Oscar **Wilson**, since the death of his wife, has concluded to leave Maryville and make his home with his son in Chattanooga. Mr. Wilson is one of the oldest citizens of this place, having lived in Maryville over sixty years. He has for several years been a deacon in the 2nd Presbyterian Church.

A Popular Event---Mr. John E. **Lutz**, the popular shoe merchant of Knoxville, and Miss Adelia **Armstrong**, of that city, were married today in the 2nd Presbyterian Church. Both bride and groom belong to the elite circles of Knoxville, and the celebration of their nuptials is one of the society events of the season. They will be at home ready to receive their friends after the 25th. The *Times* returns thanks for an invitation and extends hearty congratulations.

Mrs. W.S. **Colbert**, daughter and sons, arrived Friday evening from Indiana. Mr. Colbert went to Knoxville Friday morning to meet them. Let out citizens extend a cordial welcome and make strangers feel that they are welcome, as they always are.

In 1879, Ad **Wilson**, of this county, was arraigned before the Federal

21

Court at Knoxville for resisting the United States authorities from making a raid upon an illicit distillery in Miller's Cove. He was convicted on the charge and sentenced to twenty-one years in the United States Prison at Albany, N.Y. His conduct while in that institution was such as to warrant a pardon, and after seven years absence he has returned to his native county to gather together his family and commence life anew. A subscription paper was circulated last Thursday and Friday in his behalf to aid him in getting a home.

Cloyds Creek---Mrs. Andrew **Rose** is in a critical condition and is not expected to live.

Seaton---The work on Pleasant Grove Church is nearing completion. We think when finished will compete with any country church house. The building committee would be glad if all who have not paid their subscription would do so at once.

No Times---In the fourth Monday in Nov., a party, consisting of the following persons, viz.: L.W. **Hitch**, Andy **Hitch**, James **Harmon**, Matt. **Hitch**, William **Goddard** and A.B. **Gamble**, Jr., left here for the Smoky Mountains. We started at 4 o'clock in the morning, in high spirits, with ammunition in abundance for a week's hunt.

We reached the gap of the mountains, at Pleas **Walker**'s, by daylight; and at half past 10 we struck the foot of the Cades Cove mountains, still in good spirits, but when we got to the top of the mountain our spirits were somewhat cooled, for it was snowing on top. We cast a glance across the cove to the top of Smoky, and behold her top was white with snow when we could see a heavy fog enveloping the mountain most of the time.

Nothing daunted we pushed on and reached Mr. Cable's 15 minutes past 1 o'clock. We were expected, and so had a good dinner, to which we did ample justice, for climbing the mountain had sharpened our appetites. Here, as soon as dinner was over, we were joined by Messrs. James, Dan, Ben and Robert **Cable**.

We left our wagon and packed our grub on horses and started on foot. We went about a mile and were joined by Jule and James **Gregg**, James **Wilson**, Robert Cable (James **Cable**'s son), all on our way to get venison.

We went up the fork ridge at a rapid rate considering the steepness. It was up! Up! Up! And getting colder all the time, until there was a good tracking snow on the ground, and still snowing. We reached the cabin on the east side of the Bald just at dark, when horses were unloaded and we proceeded to get wood and made a rousing fire, after which we done justice to the bill of fare. After supping, telling yarns were in order. Jule Gregg was head man. We kept up this pastime till about midnight, when the party became drowsy and we went to bed---on the puncheon floor. About 3 o'clock next morning we were stirring, and at daylight we started for the twenty-mile flats, 3 miles southeast of the cabin---one party going down the Wolf Ridge, the other across ridges and hollows to the twenty-mile ridge, to stand for deer. The drivers had gone up above us, on the Rowan Ridge, to start game. It wasn't long until we heard the hounds coming, but instead of coming through the stands, as expected, it run around on top of the twenty-mile ridge and down the other side from us, so we did not get a shot. The drivers came on and we went to a cabin in the flats built by one **Hix**, where we made our headquarters.

The next day the deer ran off again and not a shot fired, which began to make us feel gloomy, but after the drive we had sport squirrel hunting. It was sport right, too, for you could just step out anywhere and in fifteen minutes they would be all around you.

On Thursday, Jule Gregg, the veteran deer driver, said he was going to run a deer through the stand, so we were all out early. He started one on the Rowan Ridge, which was coming right direct to the standers, on a spur of the twenty-mile ridge; and now we could hear the hounds plainly, making our hearts beat quicker, in expectation of getting a shot. On! On! It came; now it seemed as if we ought to hear the gun at the upper stand, now every ear is strained to hear a gun boom. On! On! Past the first standers, within four hundred yards of either of them, but could not be seen for the brush. Still on, and now everybody is listening for everybody else to shoot. Hark! Bang! Boom! Two shots in quick succession, and directly another; and then here comes Andy Hitch down the Wolf Ridge at a gallop to William Goddard's and Matt. Hitch's stand. Matt. Was absent but Goddard was there as soon as Andy got in hallooing distance. "Oh, Bill, have you got any buckshot?" "No," says Bill. "Where's Matt?" "He's gone to get a drink. What's the matter?" "I shot a deer down here, and I've shot all my shot away." So Bill went back with him and they got the deer. When they come in some of the boys asked Andy what he shot so much for. He said he would shoot any deer that would wink at him. From that time on we had venison.

On Friday we had set to return home, but the crowd were all for staying. We took it to a vote and all stayed except Matt. Hitch, who came home Saturday.

Saturday evening we took in the squirrels for Sunday, when we had a regular feast. Had eleven squirrels, one of the party eating eight squirrel heads.

On Monday we resumed the drive, and Tuesday we killed another deer. At 5 o'clock Thursday morning we started for home, everyone satisfied with the hunt.

Wednesday, February 17, 1886

Mrs. Mary **Frow**, wife of Thomas J. **Frow**, died of pneumonia fever, at her home 3 ½ miles west of Maryville, on Thursday morning, Feb. 11, 1886, after less than a week's sickness. On Friday afternoon her remains were carried to the Tabor church, where a very large number of friends assembled to pay their last tribute of respect to the departed. After the funeral services, conducted by pastor, Rev. E.A. **Elmore**, the corpse was quietly borne out and placed in the grave near the corner of the church.

At the age of seventeen she professed religion at a revival meeting in New Providence; but connected herself with the church at Clover Hill. When about twenty-five years old, she and Mr. **Frow** were married; and their membership remained at Clover Hill till 1871, when they withdrew to help organize the Presbyterian Church at Tabor. She manifested the deepest interest in the welfare and success of that new organization, and did what she could to preserve peace and promote piety among its members. She was by no means demonstrative, but modest, kind and good.

At home she was very industrious and thoughtful, ever looking after the comfort and happiness of her children. As a wife, she was gentle, loving and faithful, rendering her husband every assistance in her power. But her kindness was not confined simply to her own home. Her benevolence extended to the poor and afflicted, in acts of tenderest charity, and many there are who will rise up and call her blessed.

May God richly bestow his sustaining grace on the bereaved father and children, and may they be cheered with the hope of meeting her again on the evergreen.

No Time---On the night of the 7 inst., at the home of the bride's parents, Mr. James **Steele** and Miss Bessie **Nuchols** were married, Sq. **Gamble** officiating.

Louisville---The brick residence of John **Kennedy**, in Louisville, fell in last Thursday night. The building was injured during the recent cold spell. He removed his household goods in time to save most of them.

Dr. J.P. **Blankenship** received a telegram Monday morning stating that the furniture establishment of Charles **Taylor**, his father-in-law, at

Macon, Ga., was totally destroyed by fire last Saturday night. Mr. Taylor's loss is about $16,000 to be offset by $10,000 insurance.

Blount County---The old citizens give startling accounts of the suffering undergone by the first settlers of Blount County; and we read with wonder and admiration of their courage and fortitude. Their log cabins had puncheon floors, and their doors were hung with wooden hinges, and fastened by wooden latches. The furniture of their cabins was no less unpretending. The one apartment, answering the purpose of kitchen, bedroom and parlor, contained a plain home-made bedstead or two, some split-bottom chairs and wooden stools; a large puncheon supported on four legs, used, as occasion required, for bench or table; a water-shelf and bucket, a spinning wheel, and sometimes a loom.

Ramsey, in his *Annals of Tennessee*, says:

"The early occupants of log cabins were among the most happy of mankind. Exercise and excitement gave them health; they were practically equal; common danger made them mutually dependent. There was little room for envy, jealousy or hatred. To say of an individual that he was *not true*, carried with it a stigma, which, on the frontier, could never be wiped out. A new-comer to a settlement was at all times received cordially, and he and his family, if he had one, taken care of until a cabin was built for them. When this was done, the neighbors all brought them something to give them a start. A failure to ask a neighbor to a raising, a clearing, a chopping frolie, or his family to a quilting was considered a high indignity. Each settler was not duly willing but desirous to contribute his share to the general comfort and public improvement, and felt aggrieved and insulted if the opportunity to do so were withheld."

This friendly, unselfish feeling may yet be found in some neighborhoods in our county.

In July, 1795, Knox County was divided and Blount County was established, and Commissioners appointed to select a place for the county seat. The county was named for Governor **Blount**, and the county seat for his wife, Mrs. Mary Blount.

The first County Court met in September of that year at the home of Abraham **Weaver**. The first magistrates were William **Wallace**, William **Lowery**, Oliver **Alexander**, James **Scott**, David **Craig** and George **Ewing**. William Wallace was elected Chairman.

The first County officers were: James **Houston**, County Court Clerk; Robert **Houston**, Circuit Court Clerk; William Wallace, Register; Robert **Rhea**, Coroner, and Littlepage **Simms**, Sheriff.

The first settlers had to go to **Brabson**'s Ferry, twenty-two miles from

Maryville, on the Dandridge road, to do their milling, or beat their grain in a mortar. The first grist mill built in the county belonged to Mr. **Berrie**, and is now the property of Mr. W.T. **Parham**. There were quite a number of forts and block-houses built for protection from the Indians. Fort Craig was built on the hill where Capt. W.H. **Henry** and Colonel **Neff** now live; Fort **Kelly** on Mr. Peter **Brakebill**'s place, and Fort **Martin** at **Sanderson**'s Mill. Mrs. Mary **George**'s spring, some five or six miles north of Maryville, was inside **Gillespie**'s Station. This station was taken by the Indians and burned October 17, 1788, and the inmates all taken prisoners or killed. The Indians had captured a man named **Sprows**, near where the White Church now is, and told him if he would guide them to a fort or station that was not well protected they would spare his life. He took them to Gillespie's Station. After the Station was captured they made him eat dirt until he was almost dead, then shot him.

Mrs. **Henry** was on her way from Gillespie's Station to one of the neighboring forts; she was riding, and her children walking a little way before her. The Indians captured her children, but she rode back to the Station and tried to persuade the men to leave and not try to resist, for the Indians were two or three hundred strong; but they would not listen to her. While she was talking to the men, a young girl (a Miss **Hanna**) got on Mrs. Henry's horse and escaped. Mrs. Henry's plan was to go back to the Station, give them warning in time for them to escape, but to remain herself in order to be with her children. She had been captured once before and had lived with the Indians seven years. She did not live very long in captivity this time, for General **Sevier** recaptured the prisoners.

Craig's Station was at Brick Mill. Mr. **Furgason**, his daughter and a young Mr. Craig, were on their way from Craig's Station to Fort Craig, when they were surprised by the Indians. Mr. Furgason was killed, and an Indian took hold of the young lady's bridle. Young Craig rode over the Indian and seizing the young girl's bridle started back to the Station. The Indians followed. Miss Furgason's horse was frightened and finally threw her. The Indians then raising the war-whoop, sure they would capture them both; but the young man was equal to the emergency. He caught the girl and set her before him on his own horse and reached the Station in safety.

Thomas' Station was southeast of Maryville on what is now Mr. Jacob **Long**'s place. The Indians killed three men on a hill near there, and would likely have taken the Station, had not a woman called to the men in German and warned them of their danger. The men were all outside killing a beef. The Indians did not understand the woman and did not attack them immediately and they all got inside the Station in safety.

Gamble's Station was where Mr. George **Snider** now lives; and it is said that some of the logs that belonged to the old block-house may now be seen in the walls of a barn on the place. Mr. John **Walker**, a man noted for his strength and activity, usually made his home at that Station. The Indians hated and feared him and tried every way to kill him. Their secret attempts failed, and in open combat Mr. Walker was always successful. He was surprised outside the Station one evening; and as there was quite a party of the Indians they immediately made chase. They had orders not to shoot him, but to burn him. He crossed and re-crossed Crooked Creek, until he was nearly exhausted, and then crept under some laurel bushes that overhung the bank. The Indians passed and re-passed but did not find him. Next morning he went back to the Station. He never fell into the Indians' hands but lived to be a very old man.

A whole family was killed in the place now owned by Mrs. Phoebe **Tedford**, and Mr. **Wear**, father of the old Wear family living northwest of Maryville, had his house burned and all he had destroyed; but saved his life and the life of his family by escaping with them to the woods.

Mrs. **Glass** and her children were captured, and when on their way to the Indian quarters her baby became fretful and she was unable to quiet it. An Indian seized it by the feet and dashed its head against a tree, instantly killing it. They then took Mrs. Glass' apron and tore it in two; took one half, put shot in it and tied it over her shoulder, to dry up her milk; and spread the other over the dead baby and went their way.

These are only a few of the many stories that could be told about the old Indian times in our own county.

The first house built in Maryville is now occupied by Mr. John **McCollough**. Rev. Gideon **Blackburn** was the first minister, and he lived where Mrs. Susan **Kidd** now lives.

It may be interesting to the young people of the present day to know that in the olden time the young men, when skating on the ponds around Maryville, sometimes gave their lady friends a ride by pushing them before them on split-bottomed chairs.

John and Josiah **Nichols** opened the first store in Maryville, on the Lawrence corner. Dr. Edward **Gaunt** was the first physician; Messrs. John **Garner** and John **Lowery** the first lawyers.

William **Colbert** was the recipient, last week, of a fine gold headed cane from his Masonic brethren, and a Masonic pin from his Sunday School scholars, at his old home in Indiana.

The report comes to us that coal has been found near Mount Nebo, in this county. The vein is said to be four feet thick. This comes through the gas main of Knoxville.

Dr. **Jennings** is making preparations to open a street through his land, connecting the Montvale and crooked Creek roads. This is a long-felt want.

Mr. J.H. **Rogers** and family, who recently came here from Parker, Ind., have returned to their native state and will make their home at Portland.

Wednesday, February 24, 1886

Louisville Fire---Last Saturday at 1 a.m., a blaze was discovered in the drug store of Henry **Curtis**. The alarm was given and all hands joined in endeavoring to save the contents of the building. The fire soon became unmanageable. The store and residence of J.B. **Cummings** fell, victim to the spreading flames. The stock of drugs was almost an entire loss, with no insurance.

Mr. Cummings managed to save most of his stock. The fire is undoubtedly a severe loss to our neighboring town.

Friday, the barn of George **Bond**, just across the river, was burned, having been set on fire by some small children, who were playing under the wagon shed.

Gravel Branch---There was a wild horse caught near Gravel Branch last Tuesday by John **Whetsell**, John **Murr** and James **Harmon**. After running it until they were completely exhausted, James Harmon, being expert with the lasso, went home and got a rope and the fastest horse he had, and after running it about two hours finally caught it. Anyone wishing to see this wild horse can do so by calling at John Murr.

John **Morton**, who lives near the Union School house, not long since threw a stone at a chicken and killed a Jersey calf worth $20.

John **Williams** was severely rocked not long since, while going to church, by a crowd of ruffians. The parties that done the rocking were seen by persons going from church and will be identified and prosecuted to the extent of the law.

There was a party at B.B. **Steele**'s last Friday night. The little folks had a party at John **Coulter**'s last Thursday night one week ago. James **Waters** and Marion **Cresswell** got lost on going home and wandered around through the woods all night in the rain. They were so completely lost that they didn't know their nearest neighbor's houses.

Gamble's Store---Baxter **French** and Miss Maggie **Headrick** were united in the holy bonds of matrimony on last Thursday night at 6:30

p.m., at the home of the bride's parents, Mr. & Mrs. J.H. Headrick. Rev. James R. **Coulter** performed the ceremony in his usual good-natured style. We understand the happy couple were treated to some rare music the night after the marriage.

Miller's Cove---A friend informs us that Mr. John **Davis**, of Cracker's Neck, has finished the largest pair of shoes that was ever seen in the Neck. The heel measures four inches square and the whole shoe is fourteen inches in length.

Mr. James **Everett**, of Crooked Creek, and Miss Sallie **Blair**, of this Cove, were married recently at 12 o'clock by Esq. **Whitehead**. Our congratulations to them.

Blackburn **Ross** and John **Blankenship** escorted Will **Snider** to the state prison at Nashville last week.

Mrs. O.D. **Lloyd** left Saturday for Nashville, to attend the funeral of her brother, T. **Norvall**.

Mason **Evans**, the Tennessee "wild man of the mountains," who has been living in a cave in the Chilhowee Mountains for twenty-five years, was caught recently and put in a lunatic asylum.

A letter from St. Augustine, Florida by John **Collins**.

Blount County---Dr. Isaac **Anderson** was installed pastor of New Providence Church, November, 1812. He was a man of God, honored and beloved by all who knew him. The moral and religious destitution of the country distressed him greatly, and he determined to try to remedy this destitution. He wrote to the Home Missionary Societies, asking for help, but did not get it. In the spring of 1819 he was commissioned to the General Assembly, which met at Philadelphia. Before returning home he went to Princeton and visited the Theological Seminary, hoping to induce some of the young men just entering the ministry to come to East Tennessee; but he failed in this also. He came home determined to collect all the young men he could, and, in some way, educate them for the ministry. From that beginning Maryville College grew into the flourishing institution is now is. Dr. Anderson died Jan. 28, 1857. When the war began, Rev. J.J. **Robinson** was President of Maryville College, and Rev. T.J. **Lamar** and Rev. J.N. **Craig** Professors. In 1861 the troubled state of the country rendered it necessary to close the school, and it was not opened again until after the war.

29

The "Intelligencer," published by Darius **Hoyt**, was the first newspaper published in Blount County. There have been, from time to time, quite a number of newspapers started in the county, but most of them died in infancy. Let us hope the *Times* may live to a good old age. Temperance is gaining ground in Blount County. The time was when distilling whisky was considered a very respectable business, and some of the most respected citizens engaged in it; but now a whisky dealer of any kind is considered rather a questionable character. In the old militia times there was a general muster twice a year, and whisky was generally the order of the day. If there was not several drunken rows, the day was not considered a success by most of the participants. There were some exceptions, for there were order-loving men then as well as now.

During the late war the county was considerably divided. Quite a number joined their futures with the South, but the majority "stuck to the old flag." There were three companies mustered into service in the county for the Confederate Army, commanded by Captains James **McCamy**, Will **Holland** and J.E. **Toole**. Blount County was inside the Confederate lines during the first two years of the war, consequently the men that wished to enlist in the Federal Army had to slip across the lines.

Those were times that showed a man's true character. The good and bad in every heart came to the surface. Blount County had many noble men in both armies; and she had some in both that were a disgrace to her, but they were not many. The Federal soldiers came to our county for the first time on the 2nd day of September, 1863. The women and children (there was not a dozen men in the town at the time) flocked to the doors and the porches, some with bright and happy faces, and some with rather gloomy ones; but all were anxious to see what the "Yankees" looked like. One little girl, when she heard they were coming went and hid in the cellar; and when her mamma asked her why she did so, said she thought the Yankees were bears. **Woolford**'s cavalry were the first Federal troops stationed in the county, and their quiet, orderly behavior gave the citizens---even the Rebel ones---rather a good opinion of the Federal soldiers. **Wheeler** made his first raid into the county on the morning of Nov. 14, 1863. One regiment of Woolford's cavalry was still stationed at Maryville, the rest of the command having gone to Rockford. When Woolford heard of Wheeler's approach he came to meet him, but returned afterward to Knoxville, fighting all the way. That was one of the most exciting days Blount County knew during the war. A few weeks later **Sherman** came with his army. Maryville and all the surrounding county was alive with camps and camp-fires. There were more soldiers in the county at that time than at any other during the war. Gen. **Sherman** made his headquarters at Dr. **Pride**'s residence, now the Friends'

Schoolhouse. Sherman and his men did not stay long; and I do not think the people of Blount County, friends or foes, grieved much when they departed. After this a Brigade of infantry was stationed at Maryville for some time. Gen. **Beaty**, the commander, made his headquarters in the house now occupied by Mr. George **Toole**. His men, like Woolford's, were, most of them, gentlemanly soldiers. Most of the time during the winter of '63 and '64, and on into the spring, Maryville was disputed ground. Scouting parties from both armies were frequently in town the same day. When the Federal scouts came the Union ladies greeted them warmly, and always gave them something good to eat; and when the Confederate scouts came the Rebel ladies did likewise. One rainy evening a party of men rode into town, with their uniforms completely hid by rubber coats and long-topped boots. They came suddenly and from all quarters of the town. It was impossible to tell from which army they came. The men were surprised on the street corners and unable to escape. Some of the men would rather have been off the street id the soldiers belonged to the Federal Army, and some of them would have felt safer if they had been sure the scouting party were Confederates. Their look of anxious uncertainty was extremely ludicrous, and the ladies looked equally bewildered. The soldiers saw how matters stood and did not make themselves known for some time; but after awhile they exhibited their blue uniforms and went away without disturbing anyone. A company belonging to the 2nd Tennessee Infantry, and commanded by Capt. **Dorton**, was stationed at Maryville for quite a while. They made a fort of the Court House. Wheeler made his second raid in August, 1864. Capt. Dorton was still in Maryville, and he retired inside the fort with his men; when a detachment of Wheeler's cavalry, commanded by Major **Lewis**, entered the town by the Clover Hill road. Lewis was drinking, consequently was not fit for a commander. Thinking he could smoke the men out of the fort, he set fire to a house that stood just below the house now occupied by **Coning & Jones**. The wind changed and blew the smoke on the opposite direction. All the houses on the square, both east and west, were burned but three. The Court House was one of them that escaped the flames. So the Major had his trouble for nothing. The Federals held the fort until about 11 o'clock p.m. The Confederates sent for a piece of artillery and stationed it at the corner of T.P. **Cowan**'s house, on Main Street. After a cannon ball or two had passed through the fort, Capt. Dorton surrendered. The soldiers were all ordered out of town, every man of them, and not allowed to return until the next day. This was done to protect the property of the persons that had their houses burned. Most of them had, with the help of the soldiers, succeeded in getting most of their household goods out of the houses that were burned, but they did not have time to find a place to store them while the houses were burning; and after the house was gone they had nothing to protect them from the fort. The women were afraid, and whenever a soldier showed himself he was shot at from the fort; consequently, much that was left from the fire was scattered about over the vacant lots. The family then living in the house now occupied by Mr. F.M. **Watkins** was not at home. Mr. E.W. **Tedford** and one of the Confederate soldiers, thinking that house was going to burn too, resolved to try and save what was in it. It was a perilous undertaking, for they had to pass in full view of the fort for two or three hundred yards before they could reach the house. They reached it in safety, but not before several bullets had been fired at them. Some of the bullets fired at them went into the railing around the portico, and their marks could be seen only a few years ago---may perhaps be seen at the present day.

Interesting incidents of the war, and of old Indian times, in our county, are very numerous. If collected they would make quite an extensive volume.

After the war closed the College was again opened in the old buildings, on Main Street. Rev. P.M. **Bartlett** was made President, Rev. T.J. **Lamar** and Rev. A Bartlett Professors. President Bartlett set to work immediately to secure funds to erect new buildings. How he succeeded, the buildings now on College Hill bear testimony. Maryville College is a flourishing institution. There is no better in the State.

The Friends' Normal School in Maryville, is another house of learning of which any town or county might well be proud.

Porter Academy, a few miles east of Maryville, is another school that bears a good name. The public schools of Blount County are far too numerous to mention.

Blount County has quite a number of noted watering places, where the sick or weary can find health and strength breathing the pure mountain air. Our mountain scenery is unsurpassed. It is so magnificent, and so variable, that one often gets weary of admiring and is glad to enter some shady nook, where only a few laurel and ivy are visible, and then rest their ravished sight before continuing their journey over the mountains.

Blount County has a population of 18,000 (census of 1880).

Maryville is growing rapidly, and all the modern improvements, in the way of engines, farming implements and machinery of every kind, are being introduced successfully.

Many persons from the North and Northwest have come to make their homes among us. We extend to them a cordial welcome, and hope they may induce many of their friends to follow them in the near future, knowing that nowhere could they find a better place to plant a permanent home than in Blount County.

Wednesday, March 3, 1886

Some person shot through the sitting-room window of Mrs. Susan **Kidd** Monday evening. The Sheriff started in pursuit, but failed to catch the guilty person.

William **Davis**, of the 14th District, had his barn, including hay, corn, horse and farming implements destroyed by fire Monday night. The fire was undoubtedly the work of an incendiary.

A few days ago S.L. **Greer** received the sad intelligence that his son, Abraham L. Greer, had died at Toledo, Kansas, whither he had gone last April. He was taken sick on the 5th of January with inflammatory rheumatism and died on the 13th. His funeral services were held on the 15 inst., conducted by Rev. J. **Hammer**, of that place. At the time he was taken sick he was engaged in teaching school. He was a student at Maryville College for several years and was liked by all with whom he came in contact. He had made many warm friends in his new home who tendered their warmest sympathies to the bereaved parents.

We are sorry to state to our readers this week that the serial reminiscences of Blount County, of which two chapters have been published, has been discontinued. The person who has been so kind in furnishing this excellent series has our most profound thanks, and we are sure that our readers are very grateful. We are promised an article or two on Maryville, by another writer.

Elizabeth **Reagan**, an aged lady and an old citizen of this county, died Sunday between 12 and 1 o'clock, at her residence south of Maryville, of pneumonia. Her remains were interred in the Maryville Cemetery. Rev. Donald **McDonald** conducted the funeral exercises at 3 p.m. on Monday.

R.C. **Alford**, near Union Grove, died Sunday the 28th ult., in the 62nd year of his age. Mr. Alford had been an invalid for forty years.

Henry **Blevins**, of Mint, brought 800 rabbit skins to market last week. W.C. **Lane** brought 1300 the same day.

Sandy Spring---Mrs. Elizabeth **Reagan** died of pneumonia, on the 28th ult. She leaves many relatives and friends to mourn her departure.

A baptizing occurred near this place last Sabbath at 3 o'clock. Among the number was one of the oldest men in Blount County, age probably 85 years.

Flag Branch---James **Nuchols** is having the largest barn built in the 14th District. It is about 150 feet long and 60 feet wide.

Seaton---There was a wood chopping at Miss Mary **Nuchols'** Wednesday, after which the young folks spent the night in a social, while the old folks went a hunting. They all attempted to cross the foot-log with their eyes shut, and Bill **Everett** fell off and got his feet wet; he returned to the house and spent the night at the social.

Friendsville---Samuel **Greer's** oldest son died some two weeks ago in Kansas. His relatives have the sympathy of the people in their bereavement, and he has left many friends to mourn his loss.

We learn that Blount **Boring**, of this place, was badly hurt this evening by having a four horse team run away with him. He was riding one of the rear horses when they became frightened, and in attempting to leap to the ground his foot was caught and he was dragged some distance and run over by the wagon. His head was somewhat cut.

Cloyd's Creek---Mr. Amos **Hunt** expects to start to Kansas on the 8th of March, to make that State his future home.

Wednesday, March 10, 1886

A letter from Palatka, Florida by Roy **Hanna**.

Last Thursday morning Miss Retta **Wray**, daughter of J.O. Wray, died at the family residence on Washington Street. Miss Wray had been sick only a short time. The funeral services were conducted on Thursday. The bereaved family has the sympathy of the entire community in their sad loss.

Louisville---On Sunday morning, about 1 o'clock, the 21st of last month, fire was discovered in the drug store of **Curtis & Henry** but too late to save the house or contents. The dwelling house of Mr. Curtis took fire and was consumed but most of the furniture was saved. J.B. **Cummins'** storehouse was also consumed by the flames, but most of the goods were saved; no insurance. The building occupied by Curtis & Henry was rented.

South Rockford---Married at the residence of Mr. **Spears**, on the 26th of February, Mr. Isaac **Hood** and Miss **Sims**. The "old man" rather objected and there was quite a brabble for awhile.

William L. **Wrinkle** happened with a very painful, but not serious, accident last week; he went to the woods for a load of wood, cut a tree and by accident a limb fell on him, striking him on the head knocking him senseless for some time. He suffered a great deal during the night but was better in the morning, and is about straight again.

A letter from Rosendale, Missouri by J.C. **Tulloch**.

Union Grove---Our neighbor and friend, G.W. **Bishop** is badly afflicted with cancer of the mouth and is getting very low.

In Memoriam---Mrs. Kate Elizabeth **Reagan**, deceased, was of Scotch-Irish extraction.

She was born in Georgia, March 13th, 1821. When but a little girl her parents removed to Macon County, N.C., and settled near Franklin. Not long after this her parents, John and Sarah **Rogers**, removed to Blount County, Tenn., where they both died---her father, Oct, 17th, 1856, and her mother, April, 1869.

About 1839 our mother, Kate Elizabeth, came with her parents to the southern part of this county. In 1843 she married Joel Reagan---a widower---by whom she became the mother of five children---three daughters and two sons.

Mother was the third child in a family of twelve children. Being very poor, but having a powerful constitution, she raised her children, mostly, by hard laborious toil.

About the year 1870 mother became wholly dependent upon me, her only surviving son, for support and was under my care at the time of her departure.

All her surviving children were present at the time of her decease but one. Her oldest child, George W., went up from amidst her horrors of Andersonville Prison, March 14th, 1874, to join the hosts in high. She leaves four children to mourn the loss of one whose place can never be filled. At 20 minutes to 1 o'clock, p.m., Feb. 28, 1886, she took her leave of all earthly things. She lacked 13 days of being 65 years old. She died of pneumonia. She was interred in Magnolia Cemetery. Mother was a member of New Providence Church, where her three daughters are still members---all having joined during Prof. Alex **Bartlett**'s administration. ---J.T. Reagan.

35

Wednesday, March 17, 1886

A letter from Jacksonville, Florida by John **Collins**.

N. **McCoy**, J. McCoy and wife, arrived from Indiana last Friday evening and left for Allegheny Springs Saturday morning. The springs will open about May 15th. A band containing some lady musicians will be at the springs during the season to enliven the guests.

Mrs. **Kelly**, one of the oldest and most highly respected citizens of Maryville, died last Wednesday morning at 7 a.m., of cancer. She had been a constant sufferer for a long time. Her remains were interred in New Providence Cemetery Thursday. Rev. [Donald] **McDonald** conducted the funeral exercises.

The family and relatives of Henry **Miller** received a telegram Thursday morning that Mr. Miller was dangerously ill at Morristown. His son, Julius, left immediately for that point and Mrs. Miller on Friday morning. He had suffered a stroke of paralysis and very little hope of recovery was entertained from the first. Different dispatches were received, at times indicating his gradual decline. On Monday the sad intelligence came that he had died at 2 o'clock. His remains were brought home Tuesday evening and interred in the family burying ground at the old homestead. The news was a sudden shock to his friends as he had spent Sunday at home and was apparently in good health.

Seaton---Rev. J.B. **Brickey** preached Mrs. Elizabeth **Lane**'s funeral on Sunday, 14th inst., at 10 ½ a.m.

A letter from Douglas, Michigan by James M. **Anderson**.

Wednesday, March 24, 1886

In Memoriam---Died in Blount County, Tenn., Feb. 28, 1886, Robert **Alford**. The deceased was born in Sevier County in the year 1824, and removed to Blount County in 1847. He was never married until after the war, when he married Miss Sarah **Lane** and settled in the vicinity of Union Grove Church, where he remained until his death. He had not been a strong man since he was 18 years old. At that age he had fever, since when he has been afflicted with chronic disease. Eight days previous to his death he took pneumonia fever, which soon laid him to rest in the silent tomb.

Mr. Alford made a profession of religion at 20 years of age and adorned the profession he made in early life by a Godly walk through life. When he came to Blount County he joined the church by letter at Mt. Moriah, this being a Methodist Episcopal Church; afterwards he moved his membership to Shady Grove, where re remained a consistent member until called to his reward on High. In view of the rolling billows of the Jordan of death, he said he had suffered long enough and was ready and willing to die. He leaves behind him to mourn his loss an affectionate wife, who stood by his suffering couch and administered to his wants to the last; also one daughter, two sisters and a large circle of friends. After services by Rev. J.A. **Ruble** his remains were laid to rest at Big Spring.

Away from this dark world of care
He sleeps in death's cold embrace;
His soul has gone to mansions where
God's children sing redeeming grace.

The flowers of spring will open soon
Above his silent sleeping grave;
While far beyond the lonesome tomb
He blooms afresh with no decay.

The birds of spring will warble forth
Their notes of praise and joy,
While he around the eternal throne
Sings God's praise without alloy.

Then cease, ye friends, to weep and mourn
For he who has gone to rest
In that eternal, blissful home,
And on his Savior's breast.

Farewell to my devoted wife
And daughter kind and true;
Far beyond in heavenly light
I hope to meet with you.

The murder of Mrs. **Gray**, living near Loudon, by a colored man named John **Gillespie**, was a brutal transaction. He committed the deed on last Wednesday while Mr. Gray was absent attending a funeral in the neighborhood. Gillespie was found ten miles from the home of Mr. Gray. He confessed the murder, was taken to Loudon and after an examination by Mr. **Sams**, the father of Mrs. Gray, several other parties being present, he was taken by the indignant people of the county and hung to the limb of an oak tree. The real cause of the murder is supposed to be a brutal attempt to outrage the person of Mrs. Gray. Yet, when arrested, he said Mrs. Gray had told a falsehood about him. The lady murdered was a most estimable woman. There was no division in the settlement of the people, white and colored, as to the justness of the punishment meeted out to Gillespie.

Francis **Kidd**, an aged citizen of Rockford, died Sunday of pneumonia.

Francis **Kidd** died at his home at Rockford on last Saturday. He was 62 years of age. His wife is also at the point of death.

A brick foundation for the new church at Carpenter's was laid last week.

William **Means**, who lives four miles south of the city, had one thousand panels of rail fence burned Friday. The fire originated from an incendiary, a lunatic.

Arbella **Lakey**, wife of W. Lakey, at Tallassee, Monroe County, met with a serious accident Monday morning. While the husband was out attending to the feeding she had a spasm and fell into the fire, burning her left side and back into a crisp. Dr. **Garner** was called to attend her and reports the case as very critical. J.H. **Farr** brought the news to town Tuesday morning and to procure medicine.

On last Thursday night after the meeting at the Baptist church had commenced, a gentleman called Squire **Moore** to the door and informed him that he was wanted just outside the gate. The Squire followed his temporary calling and walked to the gate ajar. Being informed of their wishes he struck a match, looked at the "documents" and proceeded to pronounce Pleasant **Gentry** and Jane **Madison** as man and wife. They didn't have time to wait for the appearance of a preacher, as the "Squire advised, but wanted him to speak the words. Why the time and place of the ceremony nobody knows.

Ellejoy---Friends are sympathizing with Mr. John **Cummings** in the loss of his infant son.

Friendsville---A man by the name of **Spencer** was buried here the first of the week; some stomach trouble was the cause of his demise.
A miller by the name of **Hammon** was buried here two weeks ago tomorrow; trouble, fever.

Wednesday, April 7, 1886

Highest Water Since 1874---The continued rains of last week played havoc in all directions. Railroads, crops and fences were damaged to an almost incalculable extent. Owing to a delay in the mails a prompt and accurate report cannot be obtained.
The low lands along Pistol Creek were completely inundated.
Meadows and wheat fields were submerged and covered with a muddy sediment. The foundation under the building in the rear of the Anchor Woolen Mills was partially washed out and the building was saved with difficulty.
Every low portion of ground became a lake.
From 12 to 14 inches of water fell within 36 hours.
Louisville, in this county, was almost completely submerged, doing much damage.
The Maryville Woolen Mills were partially flooded and compelled to shut down for a short time.
Tom **Green**, colored, was drowned at **McMillan**'s while trying to rescue some parties who had been thrown from a boat.
Two piers under the railroad bridge at Pistol Creek were washed out which interrupted the passage of trains for several days. Hand cars were used in conveying passengers and freight to and from the depot to the bridge.
Little River was the scene of immense torrents, and but little fencing is to be seen along its banks. For several days it was past fording, and all the mails and passage were delayed. Alex. **Kennedy**'s saw-mill was partially destroyed and considerable lumber and lath were given up to the current.

Henry Avenue has been opened out from Pistol Creek to Washington. Gradually East Maryville is assuming the aspect of a town. The prospect is that more new buildings will be erected during this season.

Goose Neck---Our town is small---only 75 inhabitants---but we are glad to say that we have only one Democrat in the Neck.

39

Nine Mile---Gold **Wilson**, one of our best citizens, died last week. He leaves many relatives and friends to mourn his departure. His remains were laid in the graveyard at the campground.

Six Mile---Jacob **Best**, one of our members of the Sunday School and prayer meeting, has left us for Modesta, Cal. Jacob will be missed in many places, as he is a good Christian young man, and he was always ready to do his part in the Christian work. All the young people met together at his home last Friday night and enjoyed his company for the last time. A great many social enjoyments were indulged in, such as music, etc. All seemed to enjoy themselves very well. We hope if we never meet our friend again on earth, we shall meet in Heaven.

Six Mile Creek just lacked 3 feet of being as high as it was in 1875 last Tuesday evening.

Mrs. Francis **Kidd**, wife of Francis Kidd, whose death occurred only a few days since, died at her home two miles west of Rockford, Tuesday night, the 31st ult., of pneumonia fever. Her remains were interred at Mt. Moriah.

Uncle Jones **Jones**, near Friendsville, is 82 years old and has plowed every summer for seventy years without missing a single season, and intends to make a full hand at the handles this season. For his age he is a remarkable man.

Mr. Alexander **Kennedy** killed an owl last week which measured six feet and four inches from tip to tip of the wings. The bird is one of the largest of the kind ever seen. It attempted to carry off a full grown hen from the kitchen door. Mrs. Kennedy seeing the attack seizing a stick of wood and struck it.

Gone To Rest---The death of Joseph D. **Alexander**, Esq., of Loudon County, has been briefly announced in the *Times*, but it seems befitting and proper that when a good man, and one of extensive usefulness, is removed from the community by death, that the more prominent events of his life should be given for the emulation and encouragement of the rising generation.

Esq. Alexander was a son of the late James Alexander, Sr., of the Cloyd's Creek vicinity, and was born Nov. 22nd, 1828; and, having died March 23rd, 1886, was consequently in his 69th year. He was united in marriage on the 19th day of July, 1849, to Miss Lucinda **McGill**, daughter of the late Robert McGill, Rev. John **Dyke** officiating. He made a profession of religion and joined the old Baker's Creek Church in the year 1849, then under the ministration of the late Rev. Andrew **Vance**, and was soon after elected a Deacon in said church, which office he faithfully filled until the year 1871, when he, with a number of others of the membership of said church, were organized and formed the Cloyd's Creek Church, under the supervision of the late Revs. A. Vance, D.D. and William B. **Brown**; and in the year 1875 was elected and ordained a ruling Elder therein, which office he filled very efficiently and acceptably up to his death. And as an evidence of the esteem in which he was held in Kingston Presbytery to which he belonged. He was elected to represent said Presbytery in the Saratoga General Assembly, in the spring of 1879, and was also, for a number of years previous to his death, superintendent of the Cloyd Creek Sunday School. He was also elected a justice of the peace for the 7th District of Loudon County, which position he filled acceptably for ten years.

Deceased was a faithful and willing worker in the Sabbath School, the church, prayer meeting and in every place where Christian work was called for. He was ever ready to raise his warning voice to the young men against the prevalent sins and vices of the day, as well as to entreat and encourage them to embrace the religion of the Savior and to take up the cross and follow Him. As an evidence of his interest and zeal in the cause of religion, it may be stated that he aided in organizing a monthly prayer meeting among the families of Cloyd's Creek Church and for eight years previous to his illness he was never absent from one meeting, though the distance was from one to eight miles. Rain, snow, storms, heat nor cold kept him from an attendance on the means of grace or from a faithful discharge of his religious duties and obligations.

He was liberal in his contributions for religious enterprises of the day and all benevolent purposes in the community in which he lived. Take him all in all he was a model Christian and a noble citizen---one whose place will be hard to fill and who will be greatly missed.

The remains were laid to rest in the Cloyd's Creek burying ground after an appropriate service, conducted by Revs. T.J. **Lamar** and D. **McDonald**, on the 24th ult., in the presence of his bereaved widow and family and a large circle of kindred and friends.

Deceased was confined about two months with liver disease, but the dread messenger of death had no terrors for him. He died in triumph and his end was peace.

The deceased leaves four brothers surviving: Rev. J.E. Alexander of Rushsylvania, Ohio; J.D. Alexander, a former sheriff of Blount County, and at present in the railway mail service from Atlanta to Chattanooga; William J. Alexander of Cariboo, Kansas and F.M. Alexander of Loudon

County. His own family surviving consists of the widow, two daughters and three sons---all of whom are worthy members of the church, and are following in the footsteps of the sainted father and husband. "Blessed are the dead who die in the Lord."

Wednesday, April 21, 1886

Monday morning G.S.W. **McCampbell** was seated on O.D. **Lloyd** & Co.'s delivery wagon taking some barb-wire to his residence, the horse began kicking. In haste to get out of the wagon he fell under the wheels and the wagon passed over his chest inflicting a severe bruise.

Will **Love**, of this city, and Miss Annie **McCampbell**, of Loudon County, were married last Thursday eve at 6 p.m., by Rev. **Williams**. An elegant supper was served in honor of the occasion. A number of intimate friends were present to witness the ceremony. Hu. **Taylor**, of Rockford, was among the guests. Mr. & Mrs. Love arrived in Maryville Friday evening. The *Times* extends congratulations.

Mr. George **Clark**, of Yellow Sulphur, died last Saturday after several weeks of protracted illness. Mr. Clark is well known throughout the county. His death has been expected for some time and was no surprise to the public. Consumption was his ailment.

George **DeFord**, of Unitia, a crippled soldier, has just succeeded in drawing a pension amounting to $3600, and an additional bonus of $30 a month for the future.

Louisville, April 15---We are informed that Capt. **Lane** met with a misfortune yesterday by running his steamboat upon some obstruction and upset about a car-load of marble into the river.

College Notes---Mr. George **Lee**'s cow died on the Hill, east of the college last Sunday. We did not learn the cause of her death.

Wednesday, May 5, 1886

Bruce **Hardin** was accidentally shot and killed by Lum **Atchley** in the Sevierville Republican office on the 26th ult [April 26]. Lum went to his drawer, took out his pistol, walked up to the back of Bruce to examine it, when, on pulling back the hammer, his finger slipped off and the load was discharged, the bullet passing through Bruce's skull into the brain and out the forehead. This may all be so, but it is hard to reconcile it as accidental. Why Lum should find it necessary to walk up in the back of Bruce, pointing the pistol at his head in order to examine it, and in doing so kills his friend, is a little hard to understand.

Hon. Mr. **Sloof** and lady, of Jay County, Indiana, landed in Maryville on Saturday's train. Mr. Sloof will take charge of the Allegheny Springs and manage the business of the same. He has been a prominent man in his part of the State in the political world, and will be quite an addition to this soon to be famous summer resort.

Wednesday, May 12, 1886

Article containing the Tribute of Respect for Henry **Miller**.

A long letter from John **Griffitts** to his sister, Mrs. Polly **Martin**, written in 1861.

William B. **Bird**, an old and respected citizen of Tuckaleechee Cove, died on the 26th of April, 1886, in the 76th year of his age.

Deceased was born in Greene County on the 29th of March, 1811, and removed to Tuckaleechee Cove about the year 1830, and was married to Miss Susan **Campbell** on the 27th of January, 1833. They settled on the same farm where they spent all their married life, and where the widow and family yet reside. They commenced life at the bottom round of the ladder, and by industry and economy gradually accumulated a sufficiency of this worldly goods until they were enabled to raise and to give a fair English education to their large family of five sons and five daughters, who grew up to manhood and womanhood and who today survive, and all of whom are residents of the county and were present at the father's death. Two daughters died in infancy; 53 grandchildren and 18 great-grandchildren survive.

Deceased had long been a member of the Baptist Church, and when the dread messenger came he was prepared to meet him and died in triumph, exhorting his wife and children and friends to join him in the better land as long as he was able to speak and even after signified by signs that all was well.

Deceased died in perfect peace with his Maker and all mankind. And after solemn and impressive funeral services, conducted by Revs. P.B. **McCarrell** and J.D. **Lawson**, his remains were laid away in the old Tuckaleechee graveyard, April 28th, in the presence of a large circle of friends and neighbors. And thus has passed away another worthy citizen

43

of the past generation who will be greatly missed in the community in which he had so long lived.

W.C. **Chumlea** lost a fine Durham cow by death Monday night.

Miss Janie, daughter of Scott **Cox**, colored, died at Louisville last Wednesday morning of pneumonia.

Died, suddenly, at her home in the Cloyd's Creek vicinity on the night of the 8th inst., Mrs. **Alexander**, aged about 70 years. She was buried on the 9th inst., at Cloyd's Creek Grave Yard, after funeral services by Rev. J.A. **Cooper**.

Braz **Whaley**, a citizen of Sevier County, was arraigned before Commissioner **McTeer** Friday, charged with violations of the revenue law. He was discharged in this case and was immediately re-arrested on a charge of robbing the United States mail at Williamsburg, Ky. He was placed in safe keeping until the proper witnesses can be brought.

Hon. W.A. **McTeer** is in possession of an Indian battle axe which was plowed up near Fort McTeer at Ellejoy. Several years ago three persons were killed at that point by the Indians and the axe was found near the spot where the murder took place. It is thought by several in that neighborhood that the axe is the one that helped to do the bloody work.

Ida May, daughter of G.W. **Fuller**, of Springfield, died on the 6th inst. Aged one year and five days.

Joseph A. **Brown**, of Ebenezer, died Wednesday the 5th; he was in his 64th year. Funeral services at his residence conducted by Rev. J.A. **Ruble**. He was a member of the M.E. Church 39 years.

Rev. Dr.. R.W. **Patterson**, of Chicago, has been visiting Profs. **Lamar** and **Wilson** for the past few days. Dr. Patterson was baptized in New Providence Church seventy-one years ago.

He was born on the old **Strain** farm on Little River and is here visiting the scenes of his childhood.

His parents once lived on the Dr. **Anderson** farm, near Maryville, the same now occupied by Mrs. Robert **Allen**. They also lived in Knox Co. on the old Dr. Anderson farm, now occupied by S.K. **Harris**, seven miles northeast of Knoxville, and afterward near Campbell's Station.

When eight years old Dr. Patterson's parents moved to Illinois. He was educated at Illinois College and Lane's Theological Seminary at Cincinnati. Next he went to Chicago and became a pastor of the Second Presbyterian Church, when that city was a village of six thousand inhabitants, said city now numbering seven hundred thousand. This church grew to be one of the wealthiest in the United States, it being the only pastorate Dr. Patterson ever had.

In his prime he was one of the most eminent Presbyterian ministers in the North West. After resigning his pastorate in Chicago he was elected Professor in what is now called McCormick Theological Seminary and subsequently lectured for three years in Lane's Theological Seminary on "Appologetics." He is now retired. His son is managing editor of the *Chicago Tribune* and Dr. Patterson contributes to this paper.

Rockford---Samuel **Harris** died of consumption this morning about 7 o'clock, at the residence of Mr. James **Taylor**, and will be buried at Mt. Moriah tomorrow.

Wednesday, May 19, 1886

Thomas **Yearout**, aged 72, and Dolly **Lane**, aged 18, were married in Tuckaleechee Cove last Sunday by Sq. J.N. **Cameron**.

About three years ago S.B. **Rose** left Tuckaleechee for California, since which time he has been extensively engaged in farming. A few weeks ago he returned and was united in marriage to Miss Mattie A. **Cameron**, of Tuckaleechee. Mr. & Mrs. Rose left on the 8th inst., for their western home.

Our esteemed friend and brother, Dr. S.L. **Weagly**, died last Friday afternoon at 3 o'clock. On Saturday afternoon the funeral services were conducted by Rev. [Donald] **McDonald**. Several appropriate selections of Scripture were followed by a comforting talk to the bereaved family. The remains were laid to rest in Magnolia Cemetery, assisted by the Odd Fellows.

Braz **Whaley**, who was arrested a few days ago, charged with robbing the post office at Williamsburg, Ky., had a hearing before Commissioner **McTeer**, Friday and Saturday and was bound over to Federal Court.

Mr. W.A. **Hoffar**, a former resident of Blount County, but who has not been in Maryville since 1835, came over on a visit to Captain Joseph **Hood**, Saturday. He did not recognize the place for the reason that so many changes have occurred.

D.P. **Baldwin**, of Friendsville, sustained the loss of his barn by fire last Saturday, while he and his family were at church. The fire undoubtedly originated from an incendiary. The deed was committed in open daylight.

Andrew **Davis** and Miss Jennie **Hitch** were united in the holy bonds of matrimony last Saturday night near No Time, Rev. P.B. **McCarroll** officiating.

The cabins at Mount Nebo are now ready for renting at $10 for the entire season. Pay in advance. Persons desiring good accommodations should apply early. ---David **Jones**.

Mrs. [Sarah] **Ellis**, of Friendsville is 92 years of age and is now making preparation for her 57th annual May meeting.

Cloyd's Creek---Mrs. Margaret **Alexander**, whose death you noticed, was 67 years old. She died suddenly with an apoplectic fit at the house of her son, Simeon Alexander, on the night of the 8th inst. Deceased was a member of Cloyd's Creek Church. After services by the Rev. J.A. **Cooper** her remains were laid by the side of her departed husband, who died several years ago.

The *Chase County* (Kan.) *Leader* contained the following notice of the death of A.L. **Greer**, son of S.L. Greer, of Friendsville, Blount County:
"On Saturday morning, the 13th [Feb.], the many friends of A.L. Greer were pained to hear the sad but not unexpected news of his death. Mr. Greer came here from Tennessee last April and in October commenced teaching the Canaan School. He was greatly loved and respected by the pupils and patrons of the school. He was a talented young man and made many friends among the teachers of the county and seemed to have a bright future before him. But, during holidays he was taken with inflammatory rheumatism, and after five weeks of sickness passed to a brighter shore.
During his sickness he had the care of the kindest of friends and the best medical attendance, but the disease went to his heart and proved fatal. On Monday at 1 p.m. his remains were followed to the Friends' Church, the funeral sermon was preached, and then followed to their last resting place in the Friends' Cemetery by 250 or 300 people. Toledo, Safford and Canaan Schools were closed in respect to the departed, and six of the pupils from his school (Canaan) acted as pallbearers. As his remains were lowered into the grave few eyes remained undimmed for

the loss of this bright young life in the full bloom of youth, and each heart went out in sympathy for the bereaved family in their far away Tennessee home. Playmate of my youth, and friend of mature years, thou art gone; but thy memory and example remain as an emblem and a guide to a better land.

Thursday, May 27, 1886

Circuit Court commenced its usual grind Monday with a fair sized docket. Judge **Staley** in the chair. Several small cases were rapidly disposed of. As usual quite a number of petty cases were up for hearing.

The most important case, and the one that consumed the most time, was that of the State vs. Frank **Abbott**, charged with killing his father. In this case about fifty witnesses were summoned, which gave the Coves a large representation.

A Quiet Wedding---Rev. David A. **Heron**, of Elmore, Ohio, and Miss Sue S. **Walker**, of this city, were married at the residence of the bride's parents, on High Street, Tuesday, 6 p.m. Rev. E.S. Heron, father of the groom, united them in marriage. The couple will visit friends in Knox County for a few days, after which they will go to their home in Ohio. The marriage was a quiet one, only the intimate friends being present.

To The Friends Of S.L. **Weagly**, M.D., Deceased---While on his death bed it was the request of Dr. Weagly that his heartfelt thanks be returned to his many friends and neighbors, and especially to the members of the medical profession for their kind and unlimited attention given him and his family during his sickness; and that, although it was not the will of Almighty God to spare his life to return all these kindnesses, he wished his friends to know that they were most highly appreciated by him and family. ---Respectfully, Jacob Weagly.

John **Snody**, formerly a Maryville boy, returned last Thursday from Big Springs, Texas, where he located four years ago. John is postmaster at that place and is pleased with his new home. He says Maryville has made many changes for the better during his absence. He will be home about two weeks. Burrell **George** also came at the same time.

Henry **Sterling**, a well known citizen of the 6th District, died last Monday at 3 p.m., after four years of almost constant suffering. He was interred at Big Springs on Tuesday, 3 p.m., Rev. E.A. **Elmore** conducting the funeral exercises. A large number of sympathizing friends accompanied his remains to the grave. Mr. Sterling was about 60 years of age.

Horace **Heeb** and family, of California, are among the late arrivals and additions to Maryville. Mr. Heeb takes the property recently vacated by George **Huffstetler**.

Master Willie **McNabb**, of Gamble's met with a serious accident on the 19th. He accidentally got his hand into a straw cutter and had the end of his thumb ground off.

Allegheny Springs---Through the efforts of the genial proprietor, N.C. **McCoy**, the hotel at Allegheny Springs will be opened to receive guests June 1st. June 10th a grand opening will be given, for which extra preparation will be made. A grand ball will be given in honor of the occasion. The hotel building is one of the most complete in East Tennessee and is elegantly finished, with spacious halls and sleeping apartments. Its altitude makes it a place especially desirable for those who love pure air and grand scenery. Mr. McCoy assures the public that no pains will be spared to make the guests welcome, and their wants will be amply gratified.

Friendsville, May 21---Mr. **Baldwin**, whose barn was burned last week, has another erected on the same site, but of smaller dimensions.

Died, May 23rd, 1886, at her home near Maryville, Mrs. Elizabeth **Teeferteller**, wife of Joseph Teeferteller. We attended her funeral yesterday at Peck's Chapel, and not withstanding the rain quite a large congregation of sorrowing friends were present.
Mr. and Mrs. Teeferteller were the oldest couple in the county. He was a soldier in the War of 1812, and was married soon after. He claims to be 96 and his wife 92, and they were possibly over that. For about 70 years they have walked hand in hand along the lane of life.
She died saying she was going to Heaven, and exhorting children and friends to meet her there. ---J.W. **Carnes**, May 25, 1886.

Article concerning the discovery of copper and silver on the land of Pleasant **Hill**.

Wednesday, June 9, 1886

Deaths---Mrs. James **Davis** of Cracker's Neck, on June 7, of consumption. Mrs. Sarah **Bingham** of Baker's Creek, Saturday, June 5th, and she was buried at the Baker's Creek burying ground.

Gravel Hill---William **Hatcher** was thrown from a mule last week. His foot caught in the chain and dragged him about fifty yards. When he was loosed he was apparently dead, but soon after he began to breathe and was conveyed to the house.

An important suit was filed in the Chancery Court, on the 3rd inst., involving the real estate between the Montvale and Niles Ferry Road. Mrs. Ann **Pope** sues for one undivided half interest in 128 acres of the land lying as above described. Mrs. Pope is an heir and a daughter of Samuel **Pride**, deceased, who willed his property to his two children. The property became involved during the war, and was sold to pay debts. The Friends' Normal, the Freedmens' Normal Institute, Julia A.C. **Brown**, James M. **Greer**, John **Tucker**, Ben **Franklin**, D.B. **Klepper**, C.W. **Wilson**, G.W. **Huffstetler**, Daniel **Griffin**, Dennis **Johnson**, John **DeFord** are all land owners and will be involved in the suit.

A photograph has been taken of the new hotel at Allegheny Springs, Tenn., which the *Times* job office will have a fine metal cut made.

Mount Nebo opens up this week, with the genial host and hostess, Mr. & Mrs. W.M. **Murray**, in charge of the hotel.

Jim **Baxter** was hanged at Lebanon, on the 4th, for the murder of an old lady named **Lowe**.

Allen **Herbert** has been sentenced to life imprisonment at Nashville for the murder of Henry **Edwards**.

Wednesday, June 16, 1886

Linc **Houk**, well known in Maryville, was married on the 8th inst., to Miss Sue **Hudiburg**, of Knoxville. Quite a large number of presents was given to both bride and groom.

William **Ramsey** and John **Kerr**, of Sevier County, were brought in Sunday by Deputy **Freshour**, with the charge of violating the revenue law.

Rockford---Died, at his home in Rockford, on the 8th inst., Isaac L.

Henderson. His remains were interred in the Mt. Moriah graveyard.
Mr. F.M. **Vinson**, machinist at the Rockford Cotton Mills, is the father of five boys and five girls; the girls were all born on Thursdays and the boys on Saturdays.

News reached town today from Louisville that Houston **Henry**, a well known marble quarryman, was seriously injured this morning by a heavy rock falling on his right leg and crushing it. Dr. **Morton** was called to assist in dressing the wound.

In Memoriam---Another good man has gone to the spirit land. James F. **Maxwell** died at his home in VanZandt County, Texas. He was born May 2nd, 1856, in Blount County, Tenn., and was raised in said county. In 1879. He married Miss M.E. **Gholston**, of Roane County, Tenn. In 1880 he professed religion and joined the Missionary Baptist Church, of which he lived an acceptable member. In 1883 he moved to Texas, stopping in VanZandt County. His stay there was of short duration, though of the most pleasant character. He was a man that made friends by showing himself friendly. He delighted in reading and conversing on the Revelation of God; he proved by his Godly walk that there was a reality in the religion he professed; he was a man that stood upon the truth; he sought and trusted the Savior who saves to the uttermost all who comes to God by him; therefore he bore good fruit.

In the death of James Maxwell the county has lost a worthy citizen, a kind and obliging neighbor; his family an affectionate husband and father, and a loss this world cannot repay. He leaves many friends and relatives, a devoted wife and two little children to mourn his loss and to battle with the rough storms and tempests of this world without a husband's love or father's care. No doubt their loss is his infinite gain, for he died in the triumph of a living faith. Blessed are the dead that die in the Lord, henceforth, saith the spirit, they cease from their labors and their work do follow them. ---M.E. **Odell**.

Wednesday, June 23, 1886

More than ten days ago A.M. **Rule** sent his son, Jim, to the field to bring up the hay rake. The horse he took with him was supposed to be gentle and had never given rise to fear. Indeed, it was thought that the old horse didn't have energy enough to go faster than a trot. But on the return trip he broke into a run. In so doing the rake turned over and Jim was landed on the ground some distance away. His shoulder struck a tree as he fell, fracturing his collar bone. It wasn't thought that he was badly hurt, and the application of oil eased the pain. About a week later he lost the use of his arm completely. He came to the physician and then the truth dawned upon him.

Capt. **Edmondson** accidentally inflicted a painful wound last Friday which laid him up for a few days. He was trimming a small cedar bush and was holding a small limb in one hand and a knife in the other. He severed the limb. The knife was very sharp and it easily slipped and entered the left leg below the knee. The blade penetrated about an inch and a half, forcing its way between the two bones, and cutting a blood vessel. Blood poured out in a perfect stream. The wound was speedily dressed and is in itself, not dangerous.

Last Saturday, John **Franklin**, a son of Ben Franklin, was working with a pitchfork and ran a prong of the fork through the calf of his right leg. The passage was immediately in the rear of the bone. The wound is very painful and is one that will require considerable attention.

Miss Bettie **Yearout**, daughter of the late Isaac N. Yearout, died on Monday evening, of fever. She was buried on Tuesday at 2 p.m. The funeral services were conducted by Rev. E.A. **Elmore**. Her sudden death will doubtless be a surprise to her many friends.

Gravel Hill---Last Thursday as R.H. **Russell** was crossing Little River, near George **Snider**'s, his horse became frightened, slipped and fell, throwing him into the river.

Mary F. **McClure** was born in Pierson County, N.C., June 11th, 1823, and moved to this county in 1845. The deceased was a daughter of Houston H. **Phelps** and was married to Harvey B. McClure in 1848. She made a profession of religion in her 30th year, and joined the M.E. Church at Thompson's Chapel. She lived a faithful Christian until her death. She was afflicted more or less all her life, but those who were not intimately acquainted with her never knew it, as she never complained, bearing the ills of this life with patience, trying to do her whole duty in life's battle without murmuring, looking forward to life's end for her reward. She was the mother of four sons---two living, and two who have closed their eyes in death; she confidently rejoiced in the expectation of meeting them on the other shore. A week before her death she called them all around her and had them sing "I Would Not Live Always," while she shouted and told them to meet her in Heaven. She has many friends to mourn her loss, but none feel the loss so heavily as the lonely husband, who is waiting in the harvest field of time for the good husbandman to garner him with those who have gone before. May the sunlight of Heaven be his guide to that rest which remains for the people of God.

She died May 26th, 1886, lacking a few days of being 63 years old. After funeral services by Rev. P.H. **Henry**, she was buried in the Magnolia Cemetery. Many friends came to pay the last tribute of respect to an old mother in Israel, and as we looked on the last cold embraces of the grave it seemed to say to us:

> Shed not a tear for me,
> Though sorrow fill your breast,
> But pause and think in your grief
> That my soul is saved and I at rest.

> O! shed not a tear for me,
> For the pain of death is past,
> And life's long warfare closed at last,
> And my soul is saved and I at rest.

M.E. **Bowman**.

Wednesday, June 30, 1886

A Secret Wedding---Last Sunday immediately after dinner, Ike **Razor** harnessed up his horse and drove to the residence of his own and only. The two started out for a little ride. About a mile beyond Black Sulphur they met with 'Squire Will **Whitehead**, who proceeded to tie them up in the bonds of eternal connubial felicity. Of course it was premeditated on the part of the bride and groom, but neither the parents of Miss Jennie **Best**, nor those of Mr. Razor knew anything of the marriage until after the little word was spoken. Miss Best is a daughter of Christy Best, who lives near Black Sulphur.

I.A. **McCully** fell from a load of hay Saturday and broke his collar bone. The wound produced was very painful for a man of his age.

Allegheny Springs will celebrate the 4th [July] on Saturday night, 3rd, with a social dance.

Little River---Our friend, James **Houser**, while after a muskrat the other day in the creek, lost his foothold and fell in hells over head.

Article containing the Resolutions of Condolence for Dr. S.T. **Weagley**.

Will **Hodge**, near Eagleton's School-house, is very ill with consumption.

Wednesday, July 7, 1886

Allegheny Springs, formerly known as **Bogle** Springs, are situated fifteen miles from Maryville and nearly due south; and about half way up the side of Chilhowee Mountain. A commodious hotel has been erected near where the spring breaks from the mountainside, chiefly with the means and energy of Mr. Nathan **McCoy**. The hotel is in every respect complete and furnished in the best style. The rooms are all nicely carpeted and furnished with handsome walnut dressers and washstands, with marble tops and large French mirrors. The bedsteads, springs, mattresses and bed-clothing are all new. The rooms are well ventilated, and there is a noticeable absence of mosquitoes and flies; and one can take a late morning nap with the utmost enjoyment.

About forty yards up the mountain, in the rear, a large tank of five hundred barrels capacity has been erected, and is fed from a spring about a third of a mile higher up. The water is carried from the spring to the tank in pipes, and from the tank is distributed through the hotel in the same way. The fall in coming down the mountain and weight of water in the tank forces the water through the building with the power of a steam engine.

The hotel is now ready for guests and is under the present management of Mr. S.A. **Shoff**, formerly of Jay County, Indiana. Mr. Shoff is the right man in the right place, and will spare no pains to make guests comfortable. The kitchen is presided over by Mr. Samuel **Johnson**, a colored man, who is also a man of large experience, having been a cook for more than twenty years and occupied that position in some of the best hotels in the country. The kitchen is as neat and clean as any lady could wish, and the meals served could not fail to please the most fastidious.

The hotel as a health resort is all that could be desired. In the way of amusements it is at present somewhat lacking. Guests, however, can always find something in the way of entertainment; and the necessaries having been provided, the proprietor is now turning his attention to amusements. Miss Bertha **Bosworth**, a niece of the manager, is a fine performer on the piano and also a good singer, and is always willing to respond to any invitation of the guests. (But she will not dance.)

Mr. James McCoy and lady and also Mr. Peter **Danforth** and Harry **Lowe** are residents there and always ready to gratify the slightest wish of visitors.

Grassy Hollow---Will **Anderson** found a bee tree on Sim **Lane**'s farm, cut it down and got 87 pounds of honey.

Sandy Springs---Died, on last Sabbath morning, a little girl of Mrs. **Thomas**'.

Jeff **Kidd** met with an accident last Friday morning, which came near proving serious. He had harnessed his horses to his hack to start for Maryville. After seating himself in the hack and starting from the barn lot, his horses became frightened and turning suddenly upset the hack and threw him under the bed. In dragging about one hundred feet he was bruised and skinned up somewhat. The accident might have proved much more serious had he not been released just at that time.

William **Hodge**, near Rockford, whose illness we mentioned last week, died on Wednesday evening and was buried on last Thursday.

Maryville observed the 4th by keeping supremely and gloriously quiet. Not even a fire-cracker was exploded to remind us that our fore-fathers "fit, bled and died."

Mrs. Spillman, of Louisville, wife of Charles **Spillman**, deceased, died last Thursday, aged about 80 years. She joined New Providence Church under the ministration of Dr. Isaac **Anderson**.

While riding, last Thursday, Hut **Edmondson** was severely bruised by the horse stumbling and falling upon him. He was picked up in an unconscious state and at the time was thought to be fatally wounded. After careful nursing he was restored to consciousness and is out of danger, but is unable to tell how the accident occurred.

Arthur **Greer**, son of Joe C. Greer, at Yellow Sulphur, fell and broke his collar bone last week. He is doing well.

Alex **Godfrey** has succeeded in getting a pension of eight dollars a month, and back pay to the amount of $1,500.

Cloyd's Creek---Last Wednesday night, as J.E. **Klepper** was returning from Maryville, he encountered a bear family in the road near Big Spring.

Wednesday, July 14, 1886

Murder Of The Kirk Family---Nearly one hundred years ago (in 1788), John **Kirk**, a resident of what is now Blount County, accompanied by his son, set out on a journey to Knoxville, leaving his family at home, on Nine Mile Creek (Blount County) unprotected, as no fears were entertained as to their safety. During his absence his wife was terribly frightened by seeing the approach of some Indians with their hideous faces bedaubed with the war-paint peculiar to their custom. Her cry for help was unheard by any save her foes, as neighbors lived far apart in those days. Her piteous appeals for mercy were laughed at and soon stopped by the tomahawks of the red fiends. Not satisfied with the hellish work they had already done, they proceeded to murder the remaining members of the family.

Some time during the night Kirk returned, and upon entering his cabin, stumbled over the dead bodies of his family. Depict in your mind, gentle reader, the anguish of the man who had thus been deprived of all that made the pioneer's home a place of happiness. He at once set about alarming the neighbors, and incited by his request, Col. **Sevier**, who was a successful Indian fighter, organized a small force and went in search of the Indians. While crossing the Tennessee River at Citico (Monroe County), a small band of them were espied, four whom were shot and killed by Sevier's men. Thence the troops proceeded up the river to the Chilhowee towns. They again came up with a band and were forced to flee, on account of the disadvantage of an inferior force. While retreating under full gallop, Col. **Hubbard** performed the wonderful feat of shooting and killing an Indian without checking the speed of his horse.

On the same night, after Sevier's forces had camped, Corn Tassel, the acting chief of the Cherokees, accompanied by an Indian who bore the appellation of Abram, and several other Indians, came across the river under a flag. Kirk's son was a member of the troops, and as we have stated, was absent from home at the time of the murder of his relatives. Almost crazed with grief and burning with an insatiable desire to be revenged upon the treacherous foes because of their fiendish treatment of his mother, brothers and sisters, young Kirk killed the male Indians, among whom was a son of Abram, aged sixteen. Notwithstanding the Indians had never regarded the cries for mercy the white women had sent up when taken prisoners, Sevier's men, with the chivalry that was ever characterized the American pioneers, spared the lives of the women and took Abram's wife and daughter and also another squaw, with her child, who was found in the river, near the bank, with her nose and mouth just far enough out of the water to breathe. She was holding her child in the same position, and but for it would, in all probability, have made her escape. ---Written for the *Times* by Charles **Adams.**

Alex **Henry,** a wealthy colored farmer of this county, lost a good horse last week. The horse was loose in the barn yard and by some means its thigh was broken. It suffered to such an extent that Mr. Henry was compelled to end its existence.

Departed this life, on the 5th inst., George **Bishop,** for many years a citizen of the 5th District of this county. Mr. Bishop had been for years afflicted with a cancer of the mouth and suffered most excruciatingly, but expressed a confident hope of comfort and joy beyond the grave. --- J.V.I. [James Valentine **Iddins.**]

Friendsville---Aunt Sarah **Ellis** is on the sick list; she is in her ninety-fourth year. Mrs. Easter **Walker,** colored, lost a valuable cow the other day.

Letter from Clearfield, Taylor Co. Iowa written by A.B. **Ferguson.**

In Memoriam---The subject of this sketch was born in Johnson County, Tennessee; in the year 1820, was married to Sallie **Peters,** of Carter County; in 1846 removed to Blount County, where he died May 11, 1886. Daniel **Razor** was for many years a communicant in the Christian Baptist Church. With him, religion was a principle which asserted its supremacy in all the relations of life.
As a neighbor, he stood deservedly high in the esteem of the community in which he lived. He was a man of peace, ever inclined to put the mantle of charity over the foibles others, and seldom did he speak in words of sharp criticism of anyone. Now that he has passed out, his memory is cherished in affection and honor by a wide circle of acquaintances and friends. He was an exemplary citizen, and Christian patriotism was a controlling passion, causing him in all actions relating to the public to consider the good of the community at large.
In voting he was singularly conscientious, regarding the promotion of immoral men to high trusts as endorsement by the people of immorality and pernicious to the purity of the country. He withheld his support from such aspirants.
In the family relation he was a model. His was a home of domestic

felicity. He leaves a companion and six children, who feel deeply the blow that has come upon them, but also feel that the husband and father has left them a rich legacy in the pure and unsullied life that has ended here only, as we trust, to be continued in the "Grand Temple" of existence beyond. The end was but the befitting sequel of life. "Whatsoever a man soweth that shall he also reap." Having sown to the Spirit, death found him calm, resigned, triumphant and ready for the harvest soag:

When the soul from sorrow freed
Homeward hastens to return,
Mortals cry a friend is dead,
Angels shout an heir is born.

Bettie **Yearout** was born November 24th, 1861, and died June 21st, 1886.

She was confined to her room nearly three weeks. Her suffering was great. Part of the time she was unconscious.

She was converted under the preaching of Rev. P.B. **McCarrell**, and joined the Presbyterian Church and lived an exemplary life until she was called away.

She leaves a widowed mother and several brothers and sisters to mourn her loss. The Sunday School and the church will miss her; but let us rejoice to think that the church on earth has transferred another to the church above.

Although it made my heart sad when I stood by the bedside of my dying friend, knowing that her feet were touching the Jordan of death and the silver cords were loosed and the golden bowl broken at the fountain. But let us rejoice to think her soul has gone up to the paradise of God and today is waiting and watching for those of us who will soon follow.

Bettie was beloved by all who knew her; but those busy hands that brightened home are now lying in the clay, and that sweet voice is hushed in the silent tomb. How consoling to think of the victory gained by those that die in the Lord. On the day following her death she was buried in the graveyard near her home, where her father sleeps in the silent dust; so,

Sleep, Bettie, sleep;
We shed no more tears for thee,
For the pain of death is past,
And life's warfare's closed at last.

M.E. **Bowman**.

57

Wednesday, July 21, 1886

Dynamite Did It---Dynamite is a very useful article, and is almost indispensable in many kinds of work and is also quite destructive when once used amiss.

George **Anson** is a farmer living on a neat little productive mountain place in the upper edge of Cade's Cove, Blount County, near the North Carolina line.

Recently he wanted to dig a well on his place, and secured several dynamite cartridges to do blasting with. When this work was finished the remaining pieces of dynamite were placed in the upper part of a large barn, on the place, on a cross beam where they were thought to be safe. Thursday, Anson was awoke by a fearful sound and shock as though an earthquake had come around his way. Rushing out, the man found out what was, the night before, a well-filled barn, in a burning heap of ruins.

After the flames had somewhat subsided, Anson found in the ashes the charred remains of a fine cow, two horses and a mule, besides a large lot of hay and a few loads of wheat, badly damaged.

A hunt was instituted for the dynamite, but no trace of it could be found, and the supposition is that the cartridges had been knocked by a chicken and struck a wagon tire or stone beneath.

The report was heard four miles away, and during all day yesterday and Thursday many people went to see the spot where the explosion occurred.

At one end of where the barn stood was a hole in the ground about six feet square and four feet deep. ---*Journal*, July 17th.

We make note of the marriage of Dr. **Kerr**, formerly of Maryville, who is well-known in this city:

"Kerr--**Noyes**---At Canton, China, June 9, 1886, Dr. J.G. Kerr, medical missionary, to Miss Mattie Noyes, missionary.

Miss Hattie Noyes and Miss Olivis Kerr sailed from Canton, June 22, for the United States."

Bettie **Coffin** departed this life Monday afternoon, in this city. She leaves an infant still living at present writing.

Miss Adelle **Hampton**, of Memphis, is the guest of J.W. **Everett** and family. Miss Hampton visited Maryville during the summer of 1884 and made many friends, who will be pleased with her return.

"Jack" **Harmon** and James **McDonald** returned Saturday night from an extended trip to the mountains. They report a fine time, notwithstanding the most terrible storms they ever saw.

Matt **Hitch**'s little son died Monday morning of flux and fever.

Clover Hill---J.T. **Anderson**, a former resident of Clover Hill, is visiting his sister, Mrs. Clara **Hamil**, with his two motherless little ones. Jim has been in Georgia for eight years.

Sandy Springs---Mrs. J.T. **Reagan** left this place for her future home in Kentucky, July 5th. Her many friends regret her departure.

Yellow Sulphur---Willie **Huffstetler**, of Nine Mile, is the young gentleman who is running the hack from Allegheny Springs to Maryville.

Friendsville---James **Hackney**'s little boy, George, died last night. A young lady by the name of **Bowerman**, (colored), died here last week, of flux.

Wednesday, July 28, 1886

John **Miller**, of Melrose Springs, died last Wednesday morning at 9 a.m., after a lingering ailment of several weeks. He was 72 years and 7 days old. He was a member of the M.E. Church and had been an active worker for years. The funeral services were held at Piney Level on Thursday.

Roush--Gilchrist---At Chanute, Kansas, on Thursday, July 15, 1886, Mr. J. Roush to Miss Mary E. Gilchrist, formerly and for many years a well-known and highly respected lady of this place. The future home of the parties will be Rearston, Lamar County, Texas. The *Times* joins her many friends, at this place, in extending the most hearty congratulations.

Stephen **Bond**, formerly of this county, but now of Texas has been visiting friends in Blount and Knox Counties.

Ex-Dep't Sheriff John **Goddard**'s little child died of flux, Sunday morning, at Friendsville.

Miss Anna **Sharp**, of Mt. Morris, Illinois, for many years a popular society belle of Maryville, has, after an absence of several years, returned to converse with former schoolmates, of "ye olden times."

Anderson--Wear---At the residence of the bride's step-father, on the 22nd inst., in this county, by Rev. D. **McDonald**, J.T. Anderson, of Georgia, and Miss Bettie Wear, daughter of the late Robert A. Wear.

Floyd **Montgomery** passed silently into the spirit land on Monday last. Typhoid fever was the malady that burned out the life-blood. He was the son of Samuel Montgomery who was killed two years ago. His remains were interred at Pine Grove, yesterday afternoon.

Monday, August 2, 1886

Dill **Arwood**, the notorious jail-bird, and Betty **Thompson**, a woman of an unsavory reputation, engaged in a fist fight, Friday night. Betty, not satisfied with the result, swore out a warrant against Dill for assault and battery, and he submitted. Squire **Lillard** thought the peace and dignity of the state could be upheld by a fine of $10. Dill now languishes in jail---home, sweet home.

Melinda **Vance**, a colored woman, died twelve years ago. She left her clothing in a trunk, which had never been disturbed until last Wednesday when Polly Vance was taken sick. Her sister concluded to air some clothing, so the clothes of Melinda were taken out, when in the bottom was found a revolver, with six barrels all loaded, and on trial only one could be discharged.

Allegheny Springs---Are located high on the mountains, from which they derive their name. They are situated 14 miles south of Maryville, the terminus of the Knoxville & Augusta Railroad. Persons desiring to come to this resort will come via Knoxville, Tenn., and take the Knoxville & Augusta Railroad to Maryville.
To the invalid: The scenery and healthfulness of these Springs surpasses anything in the South. For pure air and pleasant nights has no equal. To those who are suffering with liver, kidney, bowel and nervous diseases, chronic chills or malarial affections, and especially those originating in the South and debilities originating from acute diseases, diseases of children and any female complaint, rheumatism, neuralgia, etc., having three kinds of water: iron, Freestone, and a spring known as the Eye Spring, for all diseases, acute or chronic.
To the Pleasure Seeker: Ample provisions will be made for dancing, to the accompaniment of stringed instruments or piano. First-class croquet

grounds. Fishing and boating near the hotel. Other amusements are fully provided for.

The Hotel---The Hotel is new and spacious, sufficient to accommodate from three to four hundred guests; is lighted with gas. Bath house, with hot or cold baths. Water on every floor. Electric call bells and fire alarms.

Livery Accommodations---A daily mail line will be run from Maryville to the Springs, with ample bus accommodations for passengers. Livery accommodations at the Hotel for persons desiring to visit the fine scenery of the region.

Medical Attendance---There will be competent physicians to attend to the wants of the sick.

Opening---The Allegheny Springs were opened June 1st, 1886. Being the first year these Springs have been opened to the public, we desire to call the attention of those who are in search of health and pleasure to test the merits of these waters.

Rates of Board---Per Day, $2.00; Per Week, $10.00 to $12.00; Per Month, $30.00 to $40.00. Special rates to families.

S.A. **Shoaff**, Manager. N. **McCoy**, Proprietor.

Houston **Henry**, a colored man of Louisville, who had his leg and ankle crushed by falling marble some time since, had his leg amputated last Tuesday by Drs. **McTeer** and **Blankenship**. Mr. Henry is doing tolerably well.

Mrs. John **Keys** died last Wednesday night, at Miser's. She ate a hearty supper and retired. Sometime during the night the family was awakened by a noise, but by the time it was located and she had been reached, her spirit had departed.

The infant son of E. **Goddard** died last Thursday and was interred in Magnolia Cemetery Friday.

A little child of Jacob **Morton** died on the 29th ult. [July 29.]

Monday, August 9, 1886

Houston **Henry**, the colored man who had his leg amputated two weeks ago, died at his home in Louisville Tuesday last.

Rev. J.A. **Ruble** dedicated the M.E. Church at Carpenter's Campground. The amount of indebtedness was provided for except $12.00. The day was not a propitious one, as it rained.

Article by Charles **Adams** concerning the 1788 Citico massacre and the burning of **Gillespie**'s Station.

Wednesday, August 18, 1886

Last Monday's train brought in a Chinaman [Ching **Wo**] from Knoxville. Having been employed at Allegheny, he was going there. The wagon in which he and his baggage were being conveyed was detained a few moments, the reporter sought an interview. We introduced ourself as well as we could and asked: "John, what trade do you follow?" After repeating several times, we got him to understand. "Chinaman do washee for Melican man. Me washeewoman." The wagon rolled away, and John bid us goodbye by throwing a kiss from the end of his nose, "Allee samee."

The residence of Arch **Farmer**, a new two-story frame, on Ellejoy, was burned last Friday. It is supposed that it was set on fire. Nothing whatever was saved. The loss, not counting household goods, is about $1,500.

James A. **Walker**, a well known young man of Miller's Cove, died last Saturday morning of consumption. His remains were interred on Sunday. The deceased had only been married about seven months.

Mrs. Sallie **Badgett**, an elderly colored woman, died of dropsy, in East Maryville, Monday night.

Allegheny Springs has secured the services of John Chinaman, **Ching Wo**, to do laundry work for visitors.

Mrs. Sophronia **Gibson**, living 4 miles east of Maryville, died on the 6th, aged 85 years. She was buried at Piney Level burying ground.

Rev. R.L. **Jenkins** will preach a memorial sermon on the death of Nancy **Hilton**, [**Helton** ?] at Antioch Church, Sevier County, the 29th of August, at 11 o'clock a.m.

Friendsville---Mr. **Scott**, who lives south of town, lost a child the first part of the week, from flux. Ephriam **Lee** lost a mare the other day from lockjaw.

Wednesday, August 25, 1886

The famous cuckoo clock, which has for years been hanging in **Tedford & Lowe**'s drug house, is to be seen no more. A Mr. **Verner**, of Texas, was in town last week, and, falling in love with the charming timepiece, purchased it. This clock has furnished amusement for all the children in the county. When striking, a bird makes its appearance in an aperture, and sings out the notes in a clear, sweet tone. There is a remarkable history connected with this clock, but we state only that it was imported from Germany probably thirty years ago; being in a Knoxville business house for a term of years, then in Maryville, and is now in Texas.

In Memoriam---Whereas, It has pleased Almighty God to remove from our midst, by death, on the 24th day of January, 1885, W.H. **Anderson**, J.P., and for forty years an attentive member of the County Court of Blount County, Tenn., a highly respected citizen of the county during his entire life of seventy-four years, and an exemplary member of the Presbyterian Church for forty-four years, the last twelve of which he was an active ruling elder, and,

Whereas, It is the unanimous desire of the court to give an expression of their feelings of esteem for their deceased associate, and of their deep affliction in his comparative sudden demise, therefore,

Resolved, That in the death of W.H. Anderson, Esq., this court has sustained great loss, the county and commonwealth a worthy, honored and most useful citizen, the church an active and exemplary office bearer, his family a kind and affectionate husband, a tender and provident father.

Resolved, That as a mark of respect for our deceased friend, these preambles and resolutions be spread upon the records of this court, and that an entire page of said records be dedicated to that use.

Resolved, That the clerk of this court be instructed to furnish a copy of this report to the wife and family of the deceased, and, also to the *Maryville Times* and *Blount County Citizen* for publication.

Adopted July Term, 1886, by the county court.

In Memoriam---Whereas, It pleased Almighty God to remove, by death, from this stage of existence, and, as we believe and trust, to a higher and happier state of being, Daniel **Rasar**, Esq., justice of the peace from the 7th Civil District of our county, on the 10th day of May, 1886, at the age of 67 years, and,

Whereas, The said Daniel Rasar was for nearly four years a member of this court, always punctual, attentive and respectful in his deportment;

Resolved, That in the death of Daniel Rasar this court has lost one of its most prompt, attentive and conscientious members, the commonwealth of the State a quiet, faithful and worthy citizen, the church a constant and exemplary member, and his family sustained the irreparable loss of a devoted and an affectionate husband, a kind and loving father.

Resolved, That in respect for the memory of Daniel Rasar, the clerk of this court be instructed to spread a copy of this report upon the records of this court, and that one entire page of said records, be devoted to that use.

Resolved, That the clerk of this court furnish a copy of this report to the wife and family of the deceased with the condolence of this entire body; and that the said clerk also furnish a copy of the report to the *Maryville Times* and *Blount County Citizen* for publication.

Adopted at July Term of county court, 1886.

The M.E. Church held its 4th Quarterly Meeting at Carpenter's Campground, in the new church, last Saturday and Sunday. Mrs. L.M. **Wells** delivered an address, Saturday evening, on temperance. The people were well pleased with her talk. At 9 a.m. Sunday Rev. J.A. **Ruble** preached the funeral discourse of Caleb **Best**; and at 11 Presiding Elder **Mann** preached an able discourse on the necessity of preparing for the Great Beyond. The sacrament of the Lord's Supper was then administered and the meeting closed.

Frank **Rogers** is lying helpless, on account of rheumatism.

William **McCully**, of west Maryville, is in a very critical condition, with fever.

Born---To Robert **Houston** and wife, a daughter, on the 16th inst.; to Bud **Hedrick** and wife, a son, on the 17th inst.; to W.A. **Coulter** and wife, a daughter, on the 6th inst. All these are grandchildren of Jacob **Niman**. Mr. Niman rejoices in the success of the Republican ticket and the arrival of three grandchildren.

Richard, youngest son of A. **Kennedy**, who lives on Little River, died yesterday morning of fever.

Bart **Wilson**, of Brick Mill, after a short sickness, died last week.

Miss M.E. **Walker**, eldest daughter of the late John Walker, died last Thursday, at the family home near Big Spring. The remains were interred on Friday. Will **Kerr**, a grandson of John Walker, is lying in a very critical condition in the same house.

A little child of Arch **Hitch** died last week at the home, about six miles northwest of Maryville. The fatal disease was flux.

Miss Neeley, a sister of John **Neely**, who lives in the Rockford district, died Friday night last.

A little child of H.L. **Wrinkle** died last Thursday near Rockford.

Mrs. William **Bird**, daughter of Alford **Seaton**, died at Line's Spring, on Sunday, the 22nd inst.

Caleb **Best**, who has had a long siege of sickness, died last Saturday morning, at his home near Carpenter's Campground. The deceased was the eldest son of the late Mike Best and was 67 years old.

Cloyd's Creek---Miss Emma **Walker** who departed this life last week, was a pious and consistent member of the Big Spring Church; had lived in peace with her family and friends and had no enemies.

In Memoriam---In memory of James **Walker**, who departed this life August the 14th, 1886, at his home in Miller's Cove.
The deceased was born January the 19th, 1867, and was the son of the late Spencer Walker, Esq. He was married December the 10th, 1885, to Ella **Coker**. They were only married eight months until God called the husband home, and the wife and two brothers are left to mourn his loss. But they do not mourn as those without hope, for the deceased was a devoted Christian. Although the last few months of his life he suffered a great deal, he never complained; he was patient unto the end. His only talk was of Heaven and its enjoyments. He was anxious to go where he would be at rest; he said he wanted to praise God.
His remains were laid to rest in the family burying ground in Miller's Cove, on Sunday the 15th inst., after funeral services conducted by Revs. W.C. **Broady** and S. **Smith**.
A devoted Christian and a kind husband has passed away. Our loss is his eternal gain. He has only gone before, and we hope to meet him soon.

In wisdom's ways we spent our days---
Much comfort we did find.
But he is gone, his race is run,

And I am left behind.
There is not a doubt upon my mind
But victory he obtained.
Although he has left me here behind
I hope we'll meet again.

From His Devoted Wife.

Wednesday, September 1, 1886

An infant child of John **Cox** died at Louisville, last Thursday.

T.N. **McArthur**, the painter at Allegheny, has gone to his home.

At Misers Station, a child of Bob **McReynolds** died of flux last Thursday.

Miss Ruhamah **McGhee** died last Monday. When called to leave this world she was 14 years old. The fatal disease was dropsy.

A son of F.R. **Potter** died at the home in Long Hollow, last Thursday night. Flux was the ailment.

Mr. Charles **Coffin**, of Texas, has been in the city for several days. Mr. Coffin is a son of John M. Coffin, who lived in Maryville about twenty years ago.

Matthew **Terrell**, wife and daughter, leave Friday morning for Oskaloosa, Iowa, to visit friends in their old home. They will remain about two months.

Rev. R.H. **Coulter** preached at the Presbyterian Church last Sunday night. Rev. Coulter left on the extra train yesterday for his home in Gallipolis, Ohio.

Mr. J. **Weagley** will depart next Monday for his old home in VanWert County, Ohio. Mr. Weagley is delighted with East Tennessee climate and will return shortly.

Mrs. Rebecca **Montgomery** died at her home about two miles east of Maryville last Sunday morning. The departed was the mother of Col. Montgomery and was aged about three score and ten.

G.A. **Cochran**, who has been at Fulda, Washington Territory, has returned to his old home near Rockford. His failure of health brought him back to Tennessee. He thinks there is no climate like the one of East Tennessee.

Five years ago, H.H. **Phelps** left Big Spring, this county, and went to Chilacco, Indian Territory. During these five years he has resided at that point.

The mother of Capt. **Rowan**, Mrs. M.N. Rowan, who lives five miles east of Maryville, was injured by a fall, last Thursday. While attempting to cross a rail fence she displaced a rail, and both fell to the ground. The injuries are not serious and no bones are broken, notwithstanding her thigh struck the rail. She is confined to her bed and is in a helpless condition. It is hoped that nothing serious will accrue.

Big Gully---On Sunday, the 15th inst., at Union Grove Church, by Rev. R.L. **Jenkins**, Anderson **Wells**, of Madisonville, to Miss Amanda **Ray**. The bride's family being opposed to her marrying, she gave them the slip by meeting her adored at the church, and, after the ceremony, going direct to Madisonville without consulting anybody. May they live long and be happy and all their responsibilities be *little ones*.

On Sunday night, 29th inst., by Rev. W.B. **Gray**, Frank **Jackson**, of Little River, to Mrs. Eliza S. **Newberry**, of Nine Mile. We congratulate Mr. Jackson on his acquisition, but his gain is somebody else's loss.

Friendsville---Mrs. William **Sexton** is still in Green County, waiting upon her father, who is quite sick.

Wednesday, September 8, 1886

A Dangerous Baptism---Toney **Thompson**, a little colored boy, was riding a very large horse from the livery stable, last Saturday. In crossing the race bridge near **Hanna** & **Thorne**'s, the horse became frightened and stepped off the bridge. As the horse fell into the water on his side, the boy sprang from the saddle and saved his life. This little fellow has had several narrow escapes in riding, but, seemingly, he is fearless.

Burned Between Two Logs---A fearful accident occurred last week at Brick Mill. Ol **Montgomery**, a well-to-do farmer of that place, was clearing a portion of his land of the old logs and rubbish. He built a large fire, with a log on either side, to hold it to its place. Mr. Montogomery owned a fine stallion, and with this animal he was dragging brush and logs to the fire. On reaching the destination with a load, the horse became entangled in the harness and was thrown into the intensely hot fire, between the two back logs. The horse was burned in a frightful manner. The fire completely demolished his eyes, burned his ears off, and not a hair was left on the creature. He was valued at $200, Mr. Montgomery having been offered that sum a short time ago.

Killed Accidentally---For several weeks, Tuck **Toole**, with a number of other colored men from Maryville, have been at work in the famous brickyards at Rockwood, Tenn. Among those who went from here was John **Lee**, a son of George Lee, who is well known in Maryville.

On last Friday Tuck and John were together in one of the brickyard shacks, a cabin of Pony **Edwards**. The two were engaged in a scuffle over a revolver. Each had a hold on the weapon and was trying to take it from the other. Soon a pistol report was heard by the men in the yards, the cabin was entered and Tuck Toole found in a dying condition.

John Lee was at once arrested. In a very few moments life had fled from Tuck and a coroners inquest was held. As there were no witnesses to the shooting, the defendant's statement was the only testimony in the case. What he stated to the jury of inquest was substantially as follows:

They were in the room together in a struggle as to which should possess the pistol. They got tired of scuffling and Tuck laid down on the bed. John, not knowing the hammer of the pistol had been raised in the struggle, pointed it at him in fun. The load was discharged and entered Tuck's head, killing him almost instantly.

The jury brought in a verdict of "accidental killing," on the testimony of the defendant.

Tuck Toole was well known in Maryville as an industrious and sober man. He was about twenty years of age. The body was brought to Maryville Saturday and was interred Sunday afternoon.

Samuel **Warren**, living near Louisville, was hewing timber with an axe, last week. In dealing a blow to the wood, the axe slipped and severed an artery in the left foot. It is a dangerous wound and will be closely watched.

The wife of George **Ray**, in the Rockford district, died of flux, Sunday morning.

Grover Cleveland, infant son of Martin and Belle **Rorax**, aged 19 months, died Sept. 3. Funeral and burial at Baker's Creek.

A child of Jim **Hicks** died Sunday morning, of flux.

Letter from Chilacco, Indian Territory written by H.H. **Phelps**.

Wednesday, September 15, 1886

At the residence of Mr. S.T. **Post**, in western Maryville, yesterday (Tuesday) morning, Herman A. **Goff** and Kittie C. Post were united in wedlock's Holy bonds, Rev. D. **McDonald** officiating. The wedding was a quiet one, none save a few of the immediate friends of the family being present.
Miss Kittie is a daughter of Mr. S.T. Post, one of Maryville's best and honored citizens. She is a charming young lady and loved and respected by everybody.
Mr. Herman A. Goff graduated from Maryville College in the year 1885, and has since been studying for the ministry at Lane's Seminary, Cincinnati. Mr. Goff was an excellent student when in college and conducted himself rightly. He is a worthy young man. Last Friday night he was ordained by the Union Presbytery as a minister of the Gospel.
The happy couple left on yesterday's train for Riceville, N.C., where Rev. Goff will assume the duties as pastor of College Hill Church. With their departure Maryville loses a cultured couple. We wish them well. May their life be the consummation of usefulness and be fraught with happiness perpetual.

Wedding Bells---Not a little speculation has been indulged in for the past few days, regarding the marriage of a popular young couple of Maryville. But last night suspicions were found to be well grounded when the bride, her sister, and the brother to the groom made their appearance.
This morning at 7 o'clock, in the parlors of the Jackson House, Mr. Joe **Burger** and Miss Lizzie **Knox** were made man and wife, Rev. P.M. **Bartlett** pronouncing the words. Immediately after the ceremony the couple took conveyance for Allegheny Springs, where they will pass a few days before returning to Maryville.
We wish Mr. & Mrs. Burger all the happiness imaginable and a successful life in every particular.

Mrs. Mary M. **Sharp**, mother of W.H. Sharp, died at her home in Maryville on the 9th inst. For five months she had been confined to her bed, when, at the age of 48 years, she was called from suffering and pain.

Miss Lucinda **Cowan**, sister to Dr. J.H. Cowan, died of consumption last Friday night. Deceased was about 60 years of age.

At Big Spring, last week, Will **Kerr**, grandson of the late John **Walker**, died at the age of about 25 years. A large number of persons attended the last exercises.

J.E. **Love**, a brother to Sam A. Love, has entered Maryville College. Mr. Love has been in Albany, Oregon, for eight years, where his mother still lives.

Two Indians were in town Monday and Tuesday from the sunny hills of North Carolina.

T.J. **Yearout** is dangerously ill with flux at his home two miles west of Maryville.

Mrs. S. **Jenkins**, of the Rockford district, departed this life, last week.

The wife of J.M. **Harris** died in the Rockford district last week.

A son of J.W. **Lane** died of flux, last week, in the 8th District.

Union Grove---William **Kerr**, of Big Spring, died on last night, after an illness of about seven weeks.
B.W. **Curtis** and L.J. **Jackson** were married on the night of the 8th and have left these parts.

Seaton---Sam **Gamble** was attacked by three dogs, near John **Riddle**'s, last Sunday night. Seeing he could not escape, Sam got up on the fence, and there he roosted until Mr. Riddle came out and drove the dogs off.

Wednesday, September 22, 1886

$4000 Worth of Enterprise---A.K. **Harper** has completed his new business house. Time and money have erected a house that a large city might be proud of. The building is a two-story brick, 90x25, and 42 feet from basement to roof. The lower floor contains about 140 feet of shelving, and will be used exclusively for boots and shoes, dry goods and groceries.

The second floor will be devoted to clothing, carpets, cloaks, window shades, etc.

A large elevator, 3500 pounds capacity, has been placed in the building and is the only one in the city.

The house is an elegant one. It does credit to the owner, to the builders and to the town in which it stands. We congratulate Mr. Harper in being sufficiently successful in business to erect such a beautiful house to accommodate his mammoth stock. We hope that he will be amply repaid for all worry and bother.

The new goods are on the road and will doubtless be ready for inspection by the time Circuit Court rolls around.

A Terrible Accident---Horace, a son of A.C. **Hafley**, of Bank, some months ago, while playing with an elder brother in his father's mill, having a rope tied to him, the rope was caught around a shaft which was then making several hundred revolutions a minute. The rope was in an instant wound around the shaft and Horace carried with the shaft at a fearful rate. But for the presence of mind and the prompt action of his brother, the revolving youth would soon have been a corpse. The water gate was closed and the only serious damage was a broken arm.

The wound healed nicely and was soon well. Last week, while playing at Porter Academy School, he fell and the arm was again broken. It was cared for by Dr. **Mullendore** and is getting along well.

T.J. **Yearout**, whose sickness we noticed in two former issues, died Thursday morning at his home two miles west of Maryville. He was 22 years of age and was an excellent boy.

Richard **Yearout**, who lived two or three miles west of town, died last Wednesday night, of fever.

A two-year old child of William **Nuchols**, died last Wednesday.

Mrs. J.B. **Tipton**, of Morganton, had her house destroyed by fore one night last week; supposed it was set on fire.

Tuckaleechee---On Friday evening our neighborhood was surprised to hear that Elizabeth **Myers** was dying. She had been suffering with rheumatism for several weeks, but was not considered dangerous. She ate a hearty dinner and then went to her son's, who lived about one hundred yards from where she lived. After walking about the house for some

71

time, she lay down. Her daughter asked her if she was sick. She answered she was not, was only tired. A few moments later she was found lying on the floor speechless. She lay till Saturday evening without speaking, when a convoy of angels bore her spirit home---there to meet her husband and children that had gone before.

Deceased was about 73 years old. She professed a hope in Christ and joined the Baptist Church at the age of fifteen. She lived a devoted Christian, always ready to reprove sin in all its forms. Her door was always open for Christian people, her ears were open to the cries of the suffering, her hands were ready to assist the sick and helpless.

We have no dying words on which to form a hope of her being in a better land, but we have over fifty years of Christian walk and Godly conversation.

She leaves nine children to mourn after her with a number of grandchildren, relatives and friends. In her death the children have lost a kind and affectionate mother, the church a faithful member, the sick a willing nurse.

Children and grandchildren, that are unconverted, may you remember the prayers she has prayed for you, may these words ever be round about you:

A mother dear has passed away,
She will greet us here no more;
But hark! I hear her singing there,
Upon the golden shore.

In Memoriam---Mrs. Sarah Rebecca **Bird**, wife of W.B. Bird and daughter of A. & M.J. **Seaton**, of No Time, Blount County, died at Lion's Springs, Sevier County, Tenn., on the 22nd day of August, 1886. She was born on the 18th of August, 1860, and was united in marriage to W.B. Bird Aug. 13th, 1879.

She professed faith in Christ in 1877, and joined the M.E. Church, at Logan's Chapel, and remained a consistent member up to the time of her death. All the days of her life on earth were 26 years and 4 days. She leaves behind a husband distressed, three little children, a sorrowing, aged father and mother, and a host of friends to mourn her loss. But with great confidence we can say that our loss is her eternal gain. She had been in a bad condition of health for some time, and for several days before her death she seemed to fully realize her condition; so death did not come to her unawares. She was ready and waiting the summons from on high. When she felt the sands of life giving away she told her mother to awake her husband and little children and let her see them all once more, "for," says she, "I will soon be gone. The angels have come and I must go." She then urged her friends to meet her in Heaven.

I would here say, for the encouragement of her friends, that I have witnessed not a few deaths but I don't know that I ever saw anyone meet death with greater resignation than did she.

> No fear, no foes dimmed that hour,
> That manifested her Savior's power;
> She leaned her soul upon his breast
> And sweetly passed away to rest.
> Asleep in Jesus, blessed sleep.
> From which none ever wake to weep,
> A calm and undisturbed repose,
> Unbroken by the last of foes.

In sympathy to all, I am, ---F.M. **Webb**.

Wednesday, October 6, 1886

Re-Arrested For Murder---In our issue of September the 8th appeared an article in reference to the shooting affair at Rockwood, Tenn. The testimony of the defendant, John **Lee**, being the only evidence given in, the jury brought in a verdict of accidental killing. The trouble arose over the disputed possession of a revolver between Tuck **Toole** and John Lee.

It seems that there are new developments in the case, sufficient for the arrest if the defendant Lee. The new evidence will be heard today at Rockwood. George Lee, father of the arrested young man and Louis **Kennedy**, left yesterday morning for Rockwood to be on hands at the trial. It is thought that a lively time will be had.

Unlawful Liquor Selling---The case of the State vs. Anson **Brooks** had a preliminary hearing before 'Squire **Lillard** Monday evening. The charge was selling liquor unlawfully. More than a score of witnesses were summoned. The evidence was sufficient to bind the defendant to a grand jury investigation.

Scott **Willson**'s child died last Saturday, after several weeks sickness.

Parent's Respect---Departed this life September the 5th, Sarah Jane, the infant daughter of William and Matilda **Tuck**. Was buried at Mt. Tabor. Aged 18 months and 26 days.

We had a darling little babe,
One that we dearly loved;
We gave her body to the grave,
Her soul to God above.
Then the loved one was taken from us.
And we bowed our heads in grief;
The day had come down for us.
And the light of our life had fled,
And we longed for the sleep of endless night,
To lay us beside the dead.

Wednesday, October 13, 1886

An Aged Man Gone---Squire Harvey **Caruthers** was taken sick with flux several months ago. Up to last Monday at about 9 a.m. he had suffered intensely.

This gentleman was 79 years of age and was raised between Maryville and Big Spring, where he has lived most of the time. In 1832 he married, but wife and children departed years ago. The funeral services were held yesterday at Big Spring Church. A note-worthy incident was the fact that the deceased was buried in the white vest which he was married in 54 years ago.

At Heiskell's Station, last week, Mr. I.A. **Bittle** and Miss Melinda **Conner** were married. On Saturday night they arrived in Maryville and passed a couple of days with the brother to the groom, Mr. J.C. Bittle.

A two year old child of Jim **Lane** died Monday evening of dyptheria.

Rev. A.F. **Whitehead**, of Huntsville, dropped into Maryville Monday evening on his way home from the Synod.

Mr. Sherard **Kithcart** returned home from Pennsylvania on Wednesday evening where he was called to see his sister in her last sickness. He arrived there on Saturday and his sister died on the Monday following.

Mr. Joseph **Frame** and sister, Miss Rebecca, left Maryville this morning for their new home in Barnesville, Ohio. Thus we lose two excellent citizens, which we very much regret.

A child of Henry **Marsh**, of Friendsville, died Monday morning.

A child of William **Craig**, of Friendsville, died Monday evening at 5 o'clock.

A Strange Incident---D.R. **Nelson** this morning dropped into the *Times* office and related a little incident of striking features.

A large house in Philadelphia, Tenn., was owned during the war by Solomon **Bogard** On the approach of General **Longstreet** with his division of the Confederates, Mr. Bogart was compelled to hide a number of articles which he wished to preserve.

A number of years afterward the house came into the possession of W.C. Nelson, father to D.R. Nelson. Last week Mr. Nelson was going to the dining room, and happened to glance at the ceiling, which by reason of age was full of cracks large enough to see through. A box met his gaze and he prized a couple of boards and secured it. The box contained eighty large plugs of tobacco. The old gentleman won't need another supply for some time, as it was well preserved. For 23 years it had been in that garret, "alone and forgotten."

A Pleasant Wedding---A very pleasant and quiet wedding takes place at 2 p.m. today, about six miles to the west of Maryville. Mr. Will F. **Hodge**, prominent young man of Morristown, and Miss Mattie A. **Dorton** are the happy parties. Rev. **Carnes**, of the M.E. Church, South, is the officiating clergyman.

Miss Dorton is a very popular young lady and is highly respected by all in the community in which she lives and also in Maryville. We congratulate Mr. Hodge on receiving as bride this lady and trust that only happiness will accrue from the union.

Louisville---Mrs. Jane **Johnston**, one of the best old ladies of our town, is seriously ill; her friends are much concerned about her condition. If it should please the Lord to take her from our midst, I believe none are more ready to obey the call of Christ. What a blessed thing to have the name in truth of a good woman.

Samuel **DeVall**, a colored man, was buried in our town yesterday. He had the character of being a peaceable, quiet and good man.

An Excellent Man Gone---Those familiar with the citizens of Maryville, and especially with the students of Maryville College, will remember the familiar features of John N. **Blackburn**, who about the year 1843-46 was a student here. He was a Jefferson County boy; had married and lived there a few years, when his wife died and he was left with two motherless children on his hands. Though surrounded with such distressing circumstances and somewhat advanced in life, the call of the Master sounded in his ears---"Go preach my Gospel"---and he "conferred not with flesh and blood" but committing his little children to the care of kind friends, he at once repaired to Maryville and entered college, and successfully prosecuted his literary course, studying theology under the venerable Rev. Isaac **Anderson**, D.D., and was licensed to preach the Gospel by Union Presbytery, in 1850. He labored for a time as an evangelist, and in the meantime was married to Miss Eliza J. **Ambrister**, a most estimable lady of this vicinity, and removed to Polk County, where he labored for a few years, for a time having charge of the Academy situated at Benton, Polk County, Tennessee. About or soon after the war he removed to Greene County, where he remained till the close of the war. In the meantime his wife had died, and he then removed to Cornersville, Middle Tenn., where he spent a year and then removed to North Alabama, where his labors were terminated a few weeks ago by a call of the Master to "Come up higher." His labors since the war were in connection with the Southern Presbyterian Church.

We are advised that he leaves a promising son in the ministry who is laboring successfully at some point in Middle Tennessee; and we are also advised that he was again married, but details of his history since the war are very meager.

A Little Excitement---A little more than five months ago Maryville was entered by a man whose name was Carnes. For about three months he was connected with the drug store of C.R. **Laughter** & Co. Commencing about the first of May he was employed by this firm as a professional prescription writer. While in Maryville he seemed to be a quiet man and was seldom seen on the streets. After being thus employed for about three months he was discharged (as his employers state) and returned to his home at Coal Creek, Tenn. He is said to have an amiable wife living at that point and three or four children. But it seems that he had rather stay at some other place; so, a short time afterward, he leaves home and family and takes up his abode in Newcomb, Tenn., as practicing physician.

On last Friday night at about 7:30 o'clock, a buggy was seen standing near the **Ferrara** building, in which the C.R. Laughter & Co. drug store now holds forth. The gentleman in question, Dr. E.C. Carnes, made his exit from the building, accompanied by Mrs. Berry **Willis**, nee Tempy **West**. The two entered the carriage and drove away and are gone. And that is all we know about it. [Compilers note: Tempy West was married to G.B. Willis on May 24, 1885. She married Elijah C. **Carnes** Nov. 10,

1887.]

Circuit Court---The adjourned session of the Circuit Court is being held in the Court House at the present. The following cases were disposed of yesterday in manner stated:

Hester V. **Madison** vs. Charles Madison, divorce; decree. Sarah **Forester** vs. Daniel B. Forrester, divorce; decree.

The greater portion of the day was devoted to the famous Dick **West** abduction case. There is considerable interest manifested in this case by our readers, it having been before them for so long a time, and hence we will give a short sketch of the case:

In October of 1885 a girl by the name of Lottie **Carter** was taken to the home of W.M. **Watkins**. A verbal agreement between Mt. Watkins and the girl was made, to the effect that she should obey as a child, should do whatsoever her hands found to do, and be recompensed by board and clothing. Previous to this engagement at Mr. Watkins', said girl had been staying at one place and another, whither her fancy attracted her; but immediately before the above contract she had been living at the home of D.R. **West**.

About seven o'clock on a morning in October, footsteps were heard by the family, who rushed to the place from whence they came. Dick West and a young man named Burgess **Ward** had hold of the girl, trying to force her from the house. Watkins and wife remonstrated but they succeeded in getting her placed on a horse at the gate and carried her away. A short distance from the house they were joined by a third, young **Bishop**, and then they rode briskly into Monroe County. Sheriff **Edmondson** was notified and started in pursuit. After fifty miles of hard riding he overtook them, arrested, and brought them back. Dick was given a preliminary trial before Esq. **Moore**, and bound over to Court. The case was continued from term to term until the present one. A large number of witnesses were introduced and interest was very great; a large number of character witnesses were also introduced.

There was nothing in the case, after all the fuss made about it. Judge **Rodgers**, in charging the jury, spoke words which could not be misunderstood. In order to be an offense as laid down by the statute, Mr. Watkins must be a parent, guardian, or legally authorized by the parent or parents of said girl. But there is no use to go further. The jury returned a verdict of not guilty.

Wednesday, October 20, 1886

Dr. H.P. **Huddleston** started to Indiana this morning to see his sister, who is very sick. Will be gone about ten days. His office will be closed while he is gone.

Mr. L.D. **Perkins**, an aged gentleman from Millers Cove, is visiting relatives in town. Mr. Perkins was born in Blount County in 1804 and has lived in the county ever since.

Rev. P.B. **McCarrell** and Rev. J.D. **Hickson** will hold a service at Mt. Lebanon Baptist Church, Oct. 24th at 11 a.m., in memory of Mrs. J.M. **Harris**. All friends of the deceased are cordially invited.

Mr. Jim **Raulston** and Miss Alice **Henry** were married last Thursday night by Rev. J.A. **Ruble**. The ceremony was performed in the middle of the road, the parties remaining in the carriage.

Little Grover Cleveland, infant son of Martin and Belle **Rorex**, of Brick Mill, departed this life Sept. 3rd, 1886, aged nineteen months and thirteen days.

"So fades the lovely, blooming flower,
Frail smiling solace of an hour!
So soon our transient comforts fly,
And pleasures only bloom to die.

Is there no kind, no lenient art,
To heal the anguish of the heart?
Spirit of grace! Be ever nigh,
Thy comforts are not made to die.

Thy powerful aid support the soul,
And nature owns thy kind control;
While we pursue the sacred page,
Our fiercest griefs resign their rage.

The gentle patience smiles on pain,
And dying hope revives again;
Hope wipes the tear from sorrow's eye,
And faith points upward to the sky."

In the afternoon, Sept. 4th, we assembled at the desolate home, and besought God to have mercy on us and make us submissive to His holy will. And at the hour of sunset we laid the little body in the grave to await the second coming of our Lord.

> "Then thou the mother of so sweet a child,
> Your false imagined loss cease to lament,
> And wisely learn to curb thy sorrow's wild;
> Think what a present thou hast sent,
> And render Him with patience what He lent."

G.S.W. Crawford.

J.T. **Price**, a brakeman on the Cincinnati Southern, while coupling cars at Chattanooga, caught his boot in the switch and was run over by the engine, killing him in only a few minutes.

John **Chitwood**, a white employee at the south Tredegar works, was struck on the head with a bar of iron by Grant **Hughes**, a colored man and almost instantly killed.

Louisville, October 13, 1886---Mrs. Jane **Johnston**, who has been dangerously ill, is reported much better, and hopes are entertained of her recovery to usual health.

In Memory of Lora **Bowman**

> Dear Lora thou art gone to rest,
> No pain disturbs thee now.
> From earth she quickly passed away,
> Death touched and chilled the brow.
> Hard it was to give her up,
> But, ah! She could not stay,
> For suddenly an angel came
> And took the flower away.

> Her kindred dear she left them here,
> To weep and mourn her loss;
> Great God in tenderness look down
> And help them bear the cross.
> It was hard to take the farewell look,
> And lay her beneath the clod;
> But she will rise above the skies
> And ever live with God.

Weep not father for thy child,
Though dear she was to thee,
From sickness, pain and suffering
She's forever more free.
Sisters and brothers why should you mourn,
Or sigh or sorrow more?
There's comfort in the blessed thought,
She's only gone before.

Her mother stands at Christ's right hand---
In joy they met on high.
How sweet to meet to part no more
And reign above the sky.
If we could just withdraw the veil
And see how blest she be,
We'd cease to sigh and weep and mourn---
God guide us unto thee.

Wednesday, October 27, 1886

A happy party assembled at the residence of J.H. **Tedford**, last
Thursday night to witness the marriage ceremony of Robert **Kidd**, son of
Jeff Kidd, and Miss Mollie Tedford, daughter of J.H. Tedford. At 6:30
o'clock about twenty-five of the nearest friends of the parties were
present and listened to the blissful words as spoken by Prof. S.T. **Wilson**.

The house of Jane **Maddox**, a poor colored woman, was burned, in the
14th District, with all she had. She had gone to see her sick daughter. She
is still away and does not know her house is burned. It is supposed it was
burned by someone. Efforts should be made to learn who these house
burners are. On the same night that Mrs. Maddox's house burned, it is
supposed the party who burned her house went to John **Holland**'s,
committed some outrages on his property.

Cards are out announcing the nuptials of Mr. C.T. **Cates**, Jr., and Miss
Emma **Parham**, at the M.E. Church South, tonight. Many friends of the
parties join with the *Times* in advance congratulations.

Wednesday, November 3, 1886

Friendsville, October 30, 1886---Frank **Endsley** was married last night
to one of Louisville's fair daughters, and his sister, Callie, and cousin,

Ratie **Lee** were missed in the school room today, having gone to the infair.

Old Uncle Charlie **Ish**, colored, was found dead in his yard the other morning; cause unknown.

Charles **Ish**, a colored man, aged 80 years fell dead Tuesday the 26th. He was not found until Wednesday. He is said to have been an excellent man. His remains were visited by all his neighbors.

Uncle Wesley **Norwood** is probably one of the oldest men in the county, and one of the most agile. He has lived under the administration of every president of the United States. Mr. Norwood cast a vote on Tuesday's election and no one challenged his vote on account of his age.

A Popular Event---The M.E. Church, South, was filled to overflowing, Wednesday night, with the select of Maryville to witness an event of much interest. Mr. C.T. **Cates**, Jr., and Miss Emma **Parham**, the union of whose hearts and hands was then to be solemnized, were ushered into the church at 6:45, followed by the approbation and good will of all present.
The ceremony was very beautiful, and was conducted by Rev. J.A. **Ruble**, the pair standing under an arch of cedar and flowers, surmounting which was a miniature sail boat.
Mr. R.A. **Kizer** and Miss Anna Parham, Mr. Joe H. **Broyles** and Miss Lula Cates were attendants; Misses Maggie Ruble and Johnnie Cates were flower girls.
The bride and groom, attendants and relatives were afterwards given a reception at the residence of the bride's father, Mr. W.T. Parham.

Boyd **McMurray**, near the Tennessee River, was badly hurt by a wild cow last Sunday. She tossed him up into a manger with her horns and then climbed up and wreaked her vengeance by standing on him. No serious injuries were done.

Will **Parham** hands us a card in which is the announcement of the nuptials of Clifton B. **Dare** and Rebecca B. **Lee**, in Indianapolis, Oct. 12th. Mr. Dare will be remembered by many Maryville persons as a student of Maryville College from 1877 to 1879. Their future home is in Minneapolis, Minn.

Mrs. **Ammons** of the 11th District, died on the 4th inst.

81

Dr. Samuel **Goddard**, of Morristown, brother to Dr. Robert Goddard, died suddenly, a few days ago.

Wednesday, November 10, 1886

Centennial Services Of Eusebia Presbyterian Church---The Centennial Anniversary of Eusebia Presbyterian Church was celebrated last Saturday and Sabbath.

On Friday the indications were very promising for a beautiful day, but early on Saturday morning a cold rain began to descend, which continued all day. In addition to this, Mrs. Dolly **Houston**, a mother in the church, who was beloved by all, was very sick and rapidly approaching dissolution. Notwithstanding these, the house was well filled on Saturday. Rev. C.B. **Lord** presided and opening, led in invoking the presence and guidance of the Holy Spirit.

Mr. John **Newman**, the leader of the choir, having been detained by the inclement weather, the music was led by Mr. John B. **Creswell**, with Mrs. Laura **McBath** presiding at the organ. Afterwards Mr. Newman and others came, when he led the choir, and Miss Aggie **Clemens** presided at the organ.

Addresses were next made as follows: Origin of the Presbyterian Church, Rev. D. **McDonald**; Introduction of Presbyterianism into East Tennessee, Prof. S.T. **Wilson**; Historical sketch of Eusebia Church, Will A. **McTeer**.

There was a large collection of relics, the most interesting of which were a glass tumbler from Germany, brought over by one of the pioneers, a Mr. **Nyman**, whose descendants are still here; a watch belonging to John **McCroskey**, one of the first Elders in the church; a sword carried through the Revolutionary, the Mexican and the late wars; a conch shell owned by Mr. Houston, one of the pioneers, which had been hid from the Indians and bleached by the soil, still kept in the family; a Confession of Faith used at the time of the organization of the church; a flax-hackle made in 1774; a pair of spoon moulds; a stone battle-axe, found on the grounds of a massacre by the Indians, near the church, together with a number of old books and other things of great interest too numerous to mention.

The weather was so bad that no exercises were held on Saturday evening.

On Sabbath Rev. W.H. **Lyle** delivered a historical sermon. It was of great value as well as interest. It should be published by all means and kept for reference by all East Tennessee Presbyterians, as well as others.

It required a vast amount of labor and careful research to collate the facts as he has done.

On Sabbath night Mr. Lyle again preached a powerful sermon, and the revival spirit manifesting itself in a powerful way, the meetings are continued.

We deem the speech of Will A. **McTeer** of much interest to our readers, hence we give below the first half, owing to its length; remainder will appear next week:

"Friends, let our present surroundings be forgotten for awhile. Imagine this whole section of country one vast forest. Not a house or field to be seen; no public roads nor improvements; tall trees sparsely set, with luxuriant grass as high as a man's shoulder, waving grandly in their shadow. In early spring or late winter the ground made clean by forest fires. Dense cane brakes along the streams where meadows now are. Herds of buffalo and droves of deer grazing quietly on hill and dale. Hungry bears prowling fearlessly here and there. Packs of wolves and crouching panthers, bold and defiant, masters of the woods. Turkeys and pheasants in innumerable hosts. The hissing viper and the warning signal of the rattlesnake, ever and anon to be heard. No man to be seen but the Indian in his most savage state; clad with skin and furs of animals, no covering for the head but tall feathers arranged in the hair; the feet protected from cold and thorns by moccasins. Armed with bow and quiver of arrows, together with the death-dealing tomahawk, and strings of human scalps suspended from the belt as trophies taken from hostile tribes. Women bearing heavy burdens, doing the drudgery, while the lazy men acted as brutal masters.

It is hard for us to realize it, but such was the condition of this country a little more than a century ago. We have many citizens who are 50 and 60 years of age, and even much older. Count back the lives of two such persons and see how short the time compared to the progress made.

Your speaker is only of the third generation by actual descent from the days of the wild state of this locality. The side of the hill, above a large flowing spring, not two miles from this place has been pointed out as the spot where Robert **McTeer** spent his first night; it was claimed to be the first for any white man on the territory that afterwards became Blount County. It was said that owls hooted, panthers screamed and wolves howled around him, until the night was made hideous and we imagine that he had considerable disturbance of his dreams. It is evident, however, that he was only one of a Scotch-Irish colony, who had escaped the oppressions of their day in the old world by coming to America; first settling in Pennsylvania and Virginia and thence coming to this place.

A fort was built, the site of which is well known, on the cleared spot, perhaps 150 yards above where **Hafley**'s Mill now stands. It was of logs, and had notches or holes cut between the logs, through which the rifles were fired, while the wall protected the body of the riflemen. These were called "port holes." This was named "**McTeer**'s Fort," and was afterwards moved a short distance and converted into a school house, in which the elections of this district were held until about the year 1867, when it was again moved and used as a blacksmith shop. The building is still standing.

The first mill of this part of the country was built near the spot where Hafley's Mill now stands, and thirty years ago there were some old men living that took delight in still abusing that old mill, because part of the machinery had to be turned by hand, and it was described as the hardest work a boy ever undertook. It was a tub mill and was washed away. In 1800 the mill was rebuilt and supplied with improved machinery, run altogether by water, but making a noise when bolting wheat that could be heard a mile, and on still days, much farther. That building, with the date of its renewal on the inside of the door, stood until after the war of 1861. During the war it ceased to operate; like Grandfather's clock, it stopped, "never to go again," and sometime after peace was made was torn down. It was a very tall log house.

Of the colony who settled here we have the names of the **Bogles**, **McCroskeys**, **McCullochs**, **McGaugheys**, **McMurrys**, **Boyds**, **Cunninghams**, **Moores**, **Houstons**, **Neymonds**, **Tiptons**, **Murrins**, **Jeffries**, **Cusicks**, McTeers and others.

These hardy pioneers were beset by dangers untold. Wild beasts were much to be dreaded, but the savage Indians were to be feared above all else. Their subtlety and deception, together with a want of openness and honesty, their blood-thirsty instincts and inhuman cruelty, made of them an enemy, from which there was no rest or permanent peace. In times when they were thought to be quiet and peaceable, parties would venture out into the surrounding country in search of game or to attend their corn.

At one of these intervals, a man named **Cunningham**, and of the family of which Major Ben Cunningham, our present Clerk of the County Court, is a descendant, went out from the fort to a place on Big Ellejoy, now in the field of Arch **Farmer**, but then covered by a tall, thick canebrake. While at or near this place, two Indians came upon him with their tomahawks, wounded him, carried him into the cane and scalped him, then left him to die. Becoming uneasy about Cunningham, a search was instituted. Two of his friends came to the verge of the canebrake, when deep, mournful groans met their ears. It was like the deception of Indians to cause these moans, hoping to draw the friends of the missing one into the cane, there to be surprised and butchered. It was like their cruelty to slowly torture a helpless victim and let him die by degrees. These brave pioneers stood, chilled and paralyzed with the situation, while the groaning rose deep and painful from the tangled mass of cane. All was still as death for a time, while these friends stood with ears set to catch the least sound. A deep, heavy moan came from the suffering man, when one of those listening exclaimed, "My God! I can't stand this!" Then rushing wildly through the cane, followed by his comrade, they bade defiance to danger and soon were beside the missing man, whom they found wounded and bleeding, but with life sufficient to tell the story of his misfortune and describe the Indians who wounded him. Cunningham was brought into the fort, but soon died. A close lookout was kept for the Indians. Pickets were posted and patrols kept on the alert. A few days after Cunningham was found, a party on a reconnoitering expedition met two Indians, just such men as Cunningham had described, in the woods along the road, between the places now owned by Jacob **Harmon** and Arch **Farmer**. They fired at once, when the small Indian fell dead on the spot, and the other, a large, active man, ran off and was traced a considerable distance by the blood that poured from his wounds. Afterwards a grave was found in Millstone Gap, on the top of Chilhowee Mountain, over which a mound of rocks was piled, where it can be found to this day. It was supposed that this was the grave of the "big brave," where he had fallen and expired from the loss of blood and exhaustion. There was a boy with the party who fired on the Indians. In retaliation the dead Indian was scalped. This boy had a knife, and asked that his knife should be used in taking off the scalp. It was done. That knife was carefully kept until a few years ago, when by deaths and changes in the family, its identity was lost.

At another time a party of three, a man named **Campbell**, his wife, and a man named **Moore**, started out from the fort to go to a station in Sevier County. Their bodies were afterward found only a short distance from where this church now stands. They had been massacred. They were buried on the spot, and their graves carefully filled. These graves have been cared for down to the present and are still preserved and watched over by kind, good people living near. Within the past year Mr. Beecher **McCampbell** found near these graves an old battle-axe, made of stone, such as was used by the Indians in the first settlement of this country. Could it speak, doubtless it could tell the bloody story of how these victims lost their lives. Its story would send a thrill of horror through this audience. On yesterday I visited the grave---for it was one grave with the three bodies interred. It is in a remarkable state of preservation. The mound over the bodies is still there, while the edge of the grave is plain to be seen, as if not of one-fourth its true age.

Frequent calls were made for men to go out after hostile bands of Indians. A story is told of one of these calls being made in mid-winter, when "Uncle Sam **Bogle**" responded. Having no shoes, he shouldered his rifle and went through frost and ice in his bare feet. The ice cut his feet until his tracks were red with blood, but without a murmur or complaint, and apparently in the very best of spirits he made the whole trip, and short would have been the life of the red man that would have come within the range of his flintlock. "Uncle Sam," as he was familiarly called, was quite a character. The old people, when I can first remember, told more of his adventures, his wit, and his peculiarities than of any other of the old men. I remember him well, when I was a child and he a very old man.

There were other trials and hardships which we can scarcely imagine. The flax and the cotton were raised, gathered, spun, woven, bleached and made into clothing all by hand, and that in the most tedious way.

Knee pants, long stockings, low shoes, claw-hammer coats or hunting shirts, with three-cornered cockades, were the fashions for men. An aged man in Sevier County, who was raised in this neighborhood, a few days ago described the hunting shirts of his early recollection. They were hand-made, of coarse woolen texture, coming down a little distance on the thighs, with belt around the waist, a loose cape falling from the shoulders, and a coarse fringe all around the borders. They were dyed in the ooze of hickory or walnut bark, as other dye stuffs could not be had.

The cooking, too, was very different from the present. Fowls were roasted on a spit, meat of animals barbecued or roasted, while there was no greater luxury than the johnny-cake, cooked on a board before the fire.

These sturdy pioneers had a strong faith in God. In these trying surroundings they looked to God as the one who could shed light in dark places.

It was no uncommon occurrence, then, for a congregation of worshipers to gather on Sabbath morning, with guns on their shoulders and large hunting knives in their belts ready for any conflict. The minister would take his position, the rifle within easy reach while he preached to the congregation.

It was of these pioneers that Eusebia Church was organized one hundred years ago. We are told that missionary meetings were held by ministers passing through the country, and this was one of the places. As nearly as can be ascertained, services were held here in that way before the organization.

The first funeral of a white person in this locality is said to have been that of a woman who came among the first and soon died. Her friends had no material for making a coffin, so a wagon bed was cut up, a rough box made of it, in which the body was placed, and her remains deposited in these grounds, which were afterwards dedicated to the public as a burying place, and for a long time were the only public burying grounds for miles around.

Another account is, that the first funeral was that of a soldier of Col. **Christian**'s command, in 1776, who was killed or died on that expedition and was buried here. We do not know which of these is the true account, but it is likely that both burials occurred as stated, and at nearly the same time.

Death Of A Young Man---The death of Mr. T.J. **Yearout** has been briefly mentioned in the *Times*. He was the eldest son of the late Isaac N. Yearout, two miles west of Maryville, and was born Oct. 22, 1864; died Sept. 16, 1886 being in the twenty-second year of age.

Deceased was a manly and sprightly young man, much respected and esteemed in the community. A few months ago his health began to decline and he was prostrated on a bed of affliction, despite the kindly nursing of his widowed mother and other friends. The death angel came and claimed him, but it is a source of comfort to the bereaved that he gave abundant evidence that he had made peace with God.

After a solemn and impressive funeral service conducted by Revs. E.A. **Elmore** and S.T. **Wilson**, his remains were laid away in the old Pistol Creek graveyard [now Cedar Point Baptist Cemetery] beside his father and sister.

Death Of Mary E. **Gilchrist**---A number of years ago there came to Maryville from Indiana a very worthy lady in a delicate state of health, named Miss Mary E. Gilchrist. Some time ago her father, Mr. A.C. Gilchrist, also came down from Indiana, and the father and daughter remained for a short time and then presuming that the California climate would best suit their feeble condition, removed to that distant state, but not being satisfied they went to Kansas, where a few months ago the daughter became acquainted with a Mr. John **Rush** of Lamar County, Texas, to whom she was married and removed to that state, where she died of consumption, on the 20th ult, [Oct. 20] in the 37th year of her age.

The many friends of the deceased in Maryville will be pained to learn of her death as she was regarded and esteemed as a most excellent Christian lady. [Mary E. Gilchrist Rush was born Aug. 12, 1848 and died Oct. 20, 1886, and is buried at Pleasant Hill Cemetery, Lamar Co. Texas.]

In Memoriam---Dr. Samuel D. **Goddard**, son of David and Matilda Goddard, of Rockford, Blount Co., Tenn., died at Morristown, Tenn., Oct. 28, 1886. He was born in the year 1858 and was 28 years old when he died. He was a twin brother to Mr. John **Lord**'s wife who crossed over on the other shore about two years ago. What a happy meeting that will be for those two who were so fond of each other here below.

He professed a hope in Christ at the age of eleven, and lived a constant Christian life up to the time of his death. He was always ready to stand up and speak a word for his Savior. He had enjoyed almost perfect health up to about a week before his death. No young man had a brighter future before him than did he. The pale messenger thrust his sickle of death into that household where it was least expected. He leaves behind him several brothers and sisters and a sorrowing father and mother.

The sad intelligence of his sudden death was severe blow on his aged parents, but when they remembered that he had lived a noble Christian life, they consoled themselves with the thought that their loss was his eternal gain. He was ready for the summons, but did not seem to realize the end so near at hand. He uttered no words in his dying hour upon which to build our hope of his being in that Heaven of rest, but we have 17 years of Christian walk and conversation to console us. He was ready at all times to reprove sin in all its forms. How mysterious are the ways of Providence, but we are sure that he in His all wise goodness, cannot do wrong. Our nearest and dearest friends pass away at the touch of the icy finger of death, but we know they are removed from us by the loving hand of Him who doeth all things well and we must be submissive to his will.

He studied medicine about the year 1879, and began the practice of the same a year later at Ebenezer, Knox Co., Tenn., and remained there about a year. From there, he went to Hot Springs, Arkansas, and was engaged in the practice of dentistry for four years, and then removed to Morristown, and continued in that profession about 15 months before he died.

He had won for himself a good name and quite a reputation in his chosen profession.

The writer extends his sympathy to that aged father and mother, brothers and sisters, in their sad bereavement. May they all meet him in that celestial land where sorrow and trouble are not known, and death and parting never come.   ---John A. Goddard, Nov. 3, 1886.

Wes **Manlove**, who came to Maryville a few months ago to follow his trade---carpentering, has sent word to his family in Spiceland, Ind., to prepare to spend the winter in Maryville.

The first snow of the season was seen, from here, on the mountains Saturday afternoon.

Mrs. Houston, of the 13th District, wife of Robert **Houston**, died Sunday, aged 80.

Louisville, November 6---Mr. Frank **Endsley** and Miss Bettie **George** was married in this city Thursday evening, 28th, [Oct. 28] at the residence of the bride's father, J.M. George, 'Squire S.L. **Greer** officiating. Miss Bettie was one among our most amiable and lovely young ladies, and the good wishes of the whole community follows her to her new home.
And on last Sunday, [Oct. 31] Mr. [S.M.] **Ball**, of Knox County, and Miss Cynthia **Hill** were married at the hotel, P.P. **Miser** officiating. Miss Cynthia has the good wishes of the citizens generally of our town. Mr. Ball, her husband, is comparatively a stranger but has the reputation of being an honest, clever gentleman.

Wednesday, November 17, 1886

Tunnell vs. Blount County---It will be remembered by our readers that J.C. **Tunnell** was arrested, several months ago, for the unlawful selling of liquor. He was on one or two cases convicted. A short time afterward Mr. Tunnell sued the county for the refunding of $300 taxes. The case had a hearing before Squire **Moore**, which Justice gave decision for the county. It was then taken before **Staley**. Here it was also decided in favor of the county. Not to be outdone, Mr. Tunnell took the case to the Supreme Court. Yesterday, the news reached us that he had again been defeated, the Supreme Court sustaining the two former Courts.

A Good Work---Rev. John **Kittrell**, of Monroe Co., has been laboring in Maryville for several days. The gentleman was homeward bound from Kentucky, where he has been conducting revival services for some time. The series of meetings began in the Friends' Church last Thursday morning and continued morning and night during the remainder of the week. Mr. Kittrell is a very earnest speaker and apparently carries with him the supreme desire of doing good to his fellow man. He preaches an excellent sermon, as those will testify who have heard him. On Sunday night New Providence Church was literally packed to hear the gentleman.

Centennial Services Of Eusebia Presbyterian Church---There is every indication that this section of country was not occupied as homes by the

Indians, but held as a great hunting ground. There were some towns in Tuckaleechee, and one on Little River, below the gap of the mountain. There was a great war-path coming down from Virginia, crossing French Broad near Buckingham's Island, up Boyd's Creek to its source, and falling upon the headwaters of Ellejoy, descended its valley to Little River, crossing, went then to the present town of Maryville, and on to the mouth of Tellico, and on down to Chickamauga. This describes the route of most of the present main road. Accordingly, about this place, the war-path turned south of the main road, descended the valley of Ellejoy to Little River and crossed the river about the mouth of Ellejoy.

Since preparing this address, I have made further inquiry and have become thoroughly satisfied that this war-path passed down the branch, about a quarter of a mile from here, by where Mr. Hugh C. **Jeffries** now lives, down the hollow to Ellejoy Creek, crossing it; then down the valley to a short distance below the mouth of Ellejoy, then crossing Little River, on to Maryville. Persons acquainted with the grounds will agree with me that a civil engineer could not locate a route more level or direct than this one.

In 1776, a body of soldiers passed through almost on the line of the war-path. The soldiers were under the command of Col. **Christian**. Rev. Charles **Cummings**, a Presbyterian minister, accompanied this expedition as chaplain. He was the first Christian minister that ever preached in Tennessee. The report of the country carried back by these soldiers brought large numbers of immigrants, all along through this section.

There was another expedition, under Col. **Sevier** (afterwards Governor) in 1782, camping at **McTeer's** Fort, now **Hafley's** Mill, on Ellejoy Creek---the English of which is Owl Creek. It was not until 1785 that McTeer's Fort was built and it appears to have been about the first fort south of the French Broad. So it was not long after the erection of a castle of defense until there was a temple of the Most High established in the wilderness.

An aged man, whose younger days were spent in this locality, says that his first recollection of Eusebia was, that it was a big log house and that, proving too small, an addition had been made to one end of the building. Most of the present generation can remember the second building, which was erected about forty years ago, and the present was dedicated Nov. 28, 1875.

For many years there was a shed and camps in the grove about 150 yards northeast of the site of the present house. I remember it well, although I was just a child, and remember that my grandfather and others watched me closely and talked in a light, child-like manner to me. The ministers sat on a platform that was near six feet high, while just below and in front of them sat six singers. It now seems to me that Messrs. James **Boyd**, Anderson Boyd and William **Creswell** were part of the singers, or Clerks, as they were then called. The platform was on the lower slope, while the congregation was seated facing it, so that the seats rose higher with the slope of the hill, as they got farther from the stand. Unfortunately the records of the church are lost down to 1832.

We have reliable information from some of our older people, that the first elders were three in number, that John **McCroskey** and Samuel **Newell** were two of them, and the name of the third is not known. John McCroskey was somewhat distinguished as an Indian fighter. There is no way to ascertain who the original members were.

On the oldest record now in possession of the Clerk there is a list of members, which starts out with the elders as follows: William **Malcom**, David **Ashmore**, John Sims, James **Upton** and James **Dunlap**, and these are marked as having been members in 1822. Then, follows a list of those who were members in October, 1822, as follows: Nancy **Malcom**, William **Snoddy**, Andrew **Creswell**, Dolly **Creswell**, Alex **McCauley**, Hetty **McCauley**, Margaret **McGaughey**, Sarah **McGaughey**, David **McCroskey**, Jane **McCroskey**, Mary **McCroskey**, John **McCroskey**, Ann **McCroskey**, Sarah **Bell**, Flora **Sheddan**, Mary **Ashmore**, Elizabeth **Creswell**, Sarah **Sims**, Nancy **Sims**, James **Boyd**, Hannah **Boyd**, William **Boyd**, Sr., Mary **McCauley**, Martha **Martin**, Nancy **Upton**, Betsy **Bogle**, Peggy **Bogle**, Nelly **Bogle**, Esther **Rhea**, Margaret **Dunlap**, Margaret **Vance**, Betsy **Ramsey**, Sarah **Cummings**, Mary **Bogle**, John **McCauley**, Polly **McCauley**, Peggy **McMurray**, Jane **Ramsey** and Joseph **McMurray**---42 members who belonged to the church prior to 1822, and were living in 1832, when this roll was made out. There were 20 additions in August and September 1823, eight of whom joined Sept. 21. (Continued)

Mr. R.J. **Cashion**, of Bonham Tex., arrived last night, to visit his sister, Mrs. **Timmons**. Mr. Cashion was a citizen of this county my years ago.

Mrs. **Catlett**, mother of Will Catlett, died last Sunday.

A daughter of N.C. **Boyd** died last Saturday.

Wednesday, November 24, 1886

The postmaster at Sevierville killed himself last week. Somebody rifled the registered mail and secured ten dollars. Being afraid that suspicion would be fastened upon him, he killed himself.

An accident is reported from Louisville, in which **Brabson**, a colored man, had his arm broken and others were slightly hurt. Later---The arm has been amputated and the man can hardly survive.

For twelve years Campbell **Gillespie**, of Little River, has been confined to his bed. Last Saturday the death angel visited his couch and relieved him of all pain and suffering. The deceased was eighty-two years of age.

Louisville---An accident is just reported from the quarry on the **Keller** farm, by the falling of a derrick. A colored man by the name of **Brabson** had an arm broken, and others slightly hurt.

Mrs. Abram **Hartsell**, familiarly known as Aunt Jane, is seriously ill. The whole community sympathizes and are sorrowful on account of her condition. She is such a noble-hearted, good woman, and all pray for her early recovery to usual health.

In Memoriam---Of Mrs. Ellen **McMurry**, who was born Oct. 2, 1800, and died Nov. 11, 1886, in Chilhowee, Monroe County, Tenn., at the residence of her son, Boyd McMurry.

The deceased had for some time been declining in health and was fully aware that she must quit the shores of time. She had been an exemplary member of the Eusebia Church for a great many years. Death seemed to have no terror for her. I frequently conversed with her; she spoke of death as one whose garments were clean and white, ready for the joyful nuptials of her nearer espousal to the Lamb. A short time before she died she repeated the Lord's Prayer audibly and also spoke of the dark rolling Jordan which was nearing. The storms of life are now past and her spirit has reached the peaceful and happy shore. It is not surprising that one who had so long walked with God should have a joyful and triumphant release from the body.

Mr. James **Carnes**, eldest son of Rev. J.B. Carnes, of Knoxville, after an absence of about seven years in Missouri, Kansas, etc., has returned and was on a visit to friends in our town a few days ago, and reviewing the scenes of his youthful days.

Kathleen **Wilson**, a daughter of Oscar Wilson, one of our prominent colored citizens, died Sunday night, aged about 17.

Wednesday, December 1, 1886

John Calvin **McCoy** Comes To His Death By Exposure---On Sunday the community was shocked to receive the intelligence that one of the oldest citizens of the county, Cal McCoy, had come to his death in a sad manner.

Saturday evening Mr. McCoy was in town. While here he became intoxicated to a great degree.

Shortly after four o'clock he started to his home, a little more than two miles on the Morganton Road. Between sunset and dark he was seen on the road near **Graston**'s. This was the last time he was seen that night.

On the next morning a search was instituted. Joe **Coleman**, living close by, was passing along the road near Seceder Church. When he came to the spring branch which flows near the road, he was attracted by several groans. Stepping to one side a few feet he beheld Mr. McCoy in an unconscious state. A little pool, or basin, had formed in the branch, and it appears that Cal had attempted to step across it, when he fell. The branch could have been crossed by a child, but owing to his unsteadiness, he fell and soon dropped into a deep slumber. His feet were in the water, but his body was on firm ground. Mr. Coleman removed a pint flask of whisky from Cal's pocket and bathed his head and pulse with the liquid, but this did not revive him.

He summoned help and removed the body to a little cabin on the hill that was built and Dr. **Blankenship** sent for. After the doctor arrived, the unfortunate man [next word unreadable] two or three times and all was over. In the evening Coroner J.P. Hackney arrived at the cabin and summoned seven jurors. The body was removed to the house of the deceased and an inquest held. The jury returned the following verdict:

State of Tennessee, Blount County---An inquisition held at the house of the deceased, in the County and State aforesaid, on the 28th day of November, 1886, before James P. **Hackney**, Coroner of said County, upon the body of John Calvin McCoy, there lying dead, by the jurors whose names are hereto subscribed, who, upon their oaths do say: That the deceased came to his death by reason of being intoxicated and falling, or otherwise getting into, a branch or basin of water, where he remained over night, from which he died shortly after being removed there from. There were no signs of violence upon the person of the deceased whatever.

John Calvin McCoy was an old and well known citizen of this county. He filled the office of County Court Clerk for two terms before the war. He was always kind, generous and good-natured. He had but one fault, and that was the one which led to his death.

Mr. McCoy was never married. He has lived with his sisters for many years. He leaves three sisters to mourn for him, all of whom are over 70 years of age, and one of them has lived for 95 years.

Mrs. Sam **Keller** departed this life at her home on Crooked Creek last Thursday, the 25th. The deceased had been ill for some time.

Will **Freshour** has gone west to grow up with the country. He started last Sunday evening. The trip will be made a short distance on horseback, and then take the train. Will's family has gone to Miller's Cove to live with his wife's mother.

A singular accident occurred to Henry **Porter**, colored, Thanksgiving evening. While playing snap at the Colored Presbyterian supper he fell, striking his head on the floor, and was rendered unconscious for the space of twenty-four hours. He was carried home, where he is improving.

Gravel Hill---It is reported that Mr. Tecumseh **Williams**, while returning from meeting the other night, run upon something he took to be a ghost. It advanced towards him with outstretched arms and wings seemingly as do the Condors of the Andes. He did not hesitate in making his escape.

Seaton---Mr. W.M. **Coulter**, of this place, has one hundred head of the finest cattle that has ever been in this community.

In Memoriam---John Calvin **McCoy** departed this life November 28th, 1886, at the age of 72 years, under circumstances calculated to move to tenderness the hardest heart and bring tears to eyes unaccustomed to weep. The circumstances of his tragic death are a warning, that those who were accustomed, with him, to drink of the flowing bowl, and all who have ever acquired the habit of indulging their appetite for strong drink, cannot afford to disregard; and are such as to excite the deepest pity and commisseration of every honest worker in the Temperance Reformation; not only for the deceased, but for all those who, like him, are, step by step and day by day, moving on to the same inevitable, mournful scene.

J.C. McCoy left Maryville for his home, three miles west of town, about dark on the 28th ult., evidently under the influence of whisky, as he frequently had done. He proceeded on his way to the old brick church, within one mile of his home; and in his attempt to cross the brook, it is supposed that he fell into the water, and, being intoxicated with a miserably poisonous article of whisky, and benumbed with cold, was unable to get upon his feet, and so lay with his feet and legs in the water during the whole of that dark, freezing night, and until 9 o'clock next day, when he was found, by a friend searching for him, in an unconscious condition, and died in a few minutes without recognizing anyone or ever speaking again.

Thus the whisky, *illegally dispensed* in Maryville, has been the direct and immediate cause of the death of a man of more than ordinary intellectual ability and an unusually large heart.

In the estimation of the writer, there never lived a man of purer or nobler impulses, and of a quicker sense of honor and gentility, by nature, than John Calvin McCoy. He was possessed of all the nobler traits of character found in weak humanity, and betrayed few, if any, of the low or mean ones. In his early life he was an ardent admirer of the esthetic, and was what might have been called, in that day, a cultivated gentleman. And although, as he himself often expressed it he was for many years "debauched and doomed, through the effects of whisky," he retained in a large degree his intellectuality, his large-heartedness, his noble impulses, his keen sense of honor and gentility, and his wonted admiration of the beautiful, to the very day of his death. But, alas! That once noble manhood was wrecked, and that pitiable wreck has been suddenly stranded and sunken by that arch-enemy of human felicity---whisky. --- W.H. Henry.

Wednesday, December 8, 1886

Last Wednesday and Thursday were as beautiful as winter days could be. On Friday night black clouds marched boldly across the heavens and gave warning of more unwelcome comings. At twelve o'clock snow began to fall and continued all night. Next morning the citizens were astonished to find about six inches of snow covering the ground. As a general thing when snow falls in this country it melts as fast as it strikes the earth. But, unfortunately, the ground was dry and frozen and each flake there remained without the loss of one.

A barn of Mrs. **McFadden**, in the Rockford District, was smashed by the weight of the snow.

Jimmie, a three year old son of Mr. & Mrs. A.K. **Harper**, died of diptheretic-croup, last Thursday afternoon. The child had been sick but a few days. The remains were interred Saturday morning.

News of a fatal accident has just reached us from Weir's Valley, over in the Smokies. On last Wednesday, Mrs. **Hedrick**, a daughter of Henry **Myers**, started from her home, on horseback, to visit a neighbor. Shortly after her departure the horse returned to the house. The saddle was displaced, the seat having been thrown beneath the horse. On searching for the woman, she was found lying in the road. Nothing definite is known as to the cause, but it is presumed that she was thrown from the animal, or that she fell off. Late in the afternoon the lady died. During the entire time between her discovery and death, she spoke not a word.

Dr. J.S. **Jenkins**, who is said to have a wife in this county, has got into trouble in his marriage to a girl in Cocke County, Tenn. He was tried before Esquire **Barnett** for bigamy and was bound over to court, and in default of bail was sent to jail. The *Times* knows of no such doctor in Blount County.

Capt. Will **Hannum** lost a barn. It is lying in the snow.

During the sickness of the little child of Andy **Harper**, Mrs. Nancy **Reagan**, of Sweetwater, the mother of Mrs. Harper, came to Maryville. On last Saturday morning at eleven o'clock Mrs. Reagan was found in an unconscious state, standing near her bed. She was immediately cared for and many friends of the family watched over her with great care. Monday morning at one o'clock her spirit left her. During her short sickness she partook of no food, and spoke not a word of comfort to the anxious watchers.

Mr. & Mrs. A.K. Harper, two of our most respected and honored citizens, have the true sympathy of the whole community in their multiplied sorrow. The *Times* wishes that the silver lining may now break upon their vision with more splendor than ever before.

Wednesday, December 15, 1886

A 100-pound black bear was killed in the 13th District, Wednesday, at the foot of the Chilhowee Mountains. John **Davis** and sons were in the field and tracked him to a little recess under a bunch of huge roots, William **Barb** soon riddled him with bullets. The question is, what was he doing so far from home.

Dr. B.A. **Morton** lost a fine horse on Saturday. His son, Ben, was riding the horse in East Maryville at a lively rate, when he fell, dashing his head against a huge rock. Later in the day the horse died. He had been bought and sold quite frequently and always brought as high as $150.

Snowballing was the favorite amusement on the streets last Saturday. Old and young alike participated. Father was arrayed against son, and brother against brother.

Squire **Lillard** had a rush of business on Monday. His Honor listened to evidence in the cases of Ben **Stafford**, larceny; Margaret Stafford, assault, and Eliza **McDonald**, profanity. The evidence was not sufficient to criminate the parties.

Sixteen barns and six houses were ruined in this county by the heavy snow.

The Snow---Later advices from the country increase the damage to barns and houses. We probably have not heard of all, but the following additional lost by the snow: Mr. **Kizer**, J.P. **Rhea**, J.E. **Klepper**, John **Williamson**, J.K. **Hair**, M.L. **Taylor**, Joe **McCall**, Mrs. **Alfred**, R.L. **Houston**, Bartley **Hafley**, and James R. **Seaton**. Three houses were demolished: E.J. **Jones**, Samuel **Jenkins**, and J.R. **Thompson**.

Rockford, December 10---We learn that several barns have been demolished by the big snow, two of which are in this vicinity---one belonging to Mrs. **McFadden** and another to Harvey **Harris**; the latter came near killing Fillmore **Spears** as it fell---an ugly gash was cut in the back of his head and neck by some of the falling timbers. Also the colored people's church, known as Walker's Chapel, fell down this week.

The new Methodist Church near Rockford is nearing completion. It is a large frame building, 38 feet wide by 56 feet long, and the walls 16 feet high. It will cost nearly $800.

It is currently reported on our streets today that Miss Esther **Merritt**, one of Rockford's fair daughters, was wedded to Mr. Jeff **Kerr** on Thursday evening.

On Monday last John **Dale** (colored), one of the top fillers at the furnace, while greasing the pulley of the hoisting engine, fell a distance of about seventy feet, breaking his neck and otherwise mangling his body, from which death at once was the result. He was one of the oldest and best hands employed by the Roane Iron Company, having worked for them about fifteen years. Dale leaves a wife and seven children. From what we can learn there is no one responsible, as it was purely an accident. The body was buried at Odd Fellows on Tuesday last, of which order he was a bright member. ---*Rockwood Times*.

The counterpart of Cal **McCoy** was found in Chattanooga last week. A man by the name of **Hagan** left Chattanooga in the evening. Next morning he was found frozen to death, with a flask of brandy beside him.

Wednesday, December 22, 1886

Last Wednesday morning the barn of Mr. H.H. **Taylor**, six miles west of Knoxville, was burned. The loss was about $2,000. There were consumed 120 load of hay, 500 bushels of corn, wagon, buggy, eleven horses, cattle, hogs, etc. It is supposed to be the work of a tramp.

A fatal shooting scrape has just been enacted a few miles above Rockwood, in which a man and boy lost their lives. A family by the name of **Wright** became enraged by the actions of one **Jackson** and had many rough words with him, when he latter procured a shot-gun and killed old man Wright and one of his sons. Jackson waived examination and was sent to jail.

Uncle Harvey **Hook**, aged about 90, is very feeble. His friends hope that he may be spared.

J.E. **Fancher** came in from Indiana Friday evening. Mr. Fancher left Maryville in February and took possession of a fine farm in Rush County.

A daughter of Rev. John **Carnes**, of Knoxville, died on Monday. A number of friends of the family went up yesterday to attend the funeral exercises.

The finest drove of hogs we have seen this year were brought in last week by John **Howard**. The average weight of the 66 was 275 pounds. Blount County is the most hoggish county in the state.

The children of Sam **Kinnamon** were playing with white beans, Wednesday. The younger one, aged 7 months, placed a bean in his mouth. In a fit of laughter the bean passed into the windpipe, from the effects of which the child died in two hours.

Much excitement has been occasioned by the development in the case tried at Louisville, Saturday, in which W.H. **Good** sued Barton **Warren**, administrator of Jared **Mead**, deceased. The case will come up at the next term of Circuit Court.

A most remarkable accident befell Dave **Eagleton**'s livestock, recently. Late in the evening a heifer ventured to cross the creek on the farm. A coating of ice formed a surface which gave way under the weight of the animal. Almost at the same time a pig made the same experiment and found a watery grave. During the night seven more hogs shared the same fate. All were drowned. Tennessee livestock is not used to skating.

What might have been a very serious accident happened to a four-year old daughter of Dan **Bird**, last Saturday. A son of Mr. Bird was trying to split a large stick of wood, and the little girl was playing very nearby. Something interrupted her balance, and she fell before him, just as the ax was again coming to the chunk. The blade struck the child perpendicular across the center of the forehead, cutting a terrible gash between the eyes. It is a very unhappy occurrence, but it will hardly prove of a serious nature.

Friendsville, December 17---Two degrees below zero this morning. Frank **Sexton** trimmed a coffin yesterday for a man by the name of **Holland**, near Concord, who died from the effects of a fall a few days ago. He was unconscious all the time.

John **Donaldson** and brother, who have been holding claims in Western Kansas, returned last week, being perfectly convinced that there is no place like home.

Louisville---The sad news of the death of Mr. James **Holland** has just been received. Mr. Holland lived in **Taliferro**'s Bend, about 5 miles below here, on the Tennessee River. He was a clever, honest man, a good citizen, and his death is generally deplored.

College Notes---The few old friends remaining in the community were much surprised and gratified to meet Rev. P.C. **Baldwin**, who spent a day in our town last week. He was educated at the Southern & Western Theological Seminary, which has merged into Maryville College. He also studied Theology under the late Rev. Isaac **Anderson** and was for a few years an inmate of Dr. Anderson's family. He came to Maryville in the year 1837 and remained here six or eight years. He is now, and has been for some time, a minister of the Presbyterian Church and located at South Toledo, Ohio.

Wednesday, October 5, 1887

Burned To Death---A little child, two years old, of John **Waters**, at Seaton, Sunday night, while attempting to lift a lamp off a table caught its clothes on fire and before assistance could be rendered the child was very badly burned and died from the effects.

Railroad Accident---On Friday at Knoxville, William **Henry**, an esteemed and industrious colored brakeman on the K. & A. Railroad, was coupling cars. While standing on the rail signaling the other brakeman to come back further the engine came back very suddenly, catching him in the hips. The cars were these coal cars with the frames projecting at the corners. The place of the accident was on a curve and the engineer could not see where Henry was standing. Later: Mr. Henry died Saturday from the effects of his injuries. The funeral took place at his home in West Maryville, Sunday at 2 o'clock.

The inside of the Court House was nicely decorated with mottoes near the place of voting. Voters passed under and between them to go to the ballot-box so that they could read, "Vote for God, vote for home and our boys."

College Notes---Prof. **Wilson** returned on Thursday last from the funeral of his father. He had to hurry back to get here in time to vote. His father, when on his death bed, mistook the day, and thought the election day had arrived, and he wanted to be carried to the polls to vote for the Amendment, and looked disappointed when told that the election would be a week later. He knew he could not live that long. Mr. Wilson was, all his life through, a self-sacrificing philanthropist. Although still weary from a week of watching and anxiety, Prof. Wilson met his classes on Monday morning.

The Crime Of Arson---The trial of the Rev. E. Winston **Taylor** for the burning of the parsonage of the A.M.E.Z. Church at this place last April, and Thomas **Snider** for complicity in same, engaged the Court on Thursday afternoon, all day Friday and Saturday. There were two counts in the indictment. In the first count Taylor was found guilty and given 8 years in the "pen" and Snider 6 years. In the second count Taylor got 5 years more and Snider 1 year. The total years of imprisonment gives Taylor 13 and Snider 7.

The evidence was conclusive and the jury found them guilty. The counsel for the defense made a desperate effort to save their clients but the evidence was too strong.

The case of Isaac **Hood** for the burning of Mr. **Davis'** barn near Rockford, one year ago last January, was tried at this term of court. This case has been continued from court to court, the defendant being on bond. The evidence was all circumstantial, except that William **McAffry**, a detective, who swore that Hood had confessed to the burning of the barn. On this evidence of Hood making threats to get even with Davis, the state relied.

J.C.J. **Williams** of Knoxville appeared for the state and Thomas **Brown** and R.N. Hood for the defense, who relied on an alibi to some extent.

The jury returned a verdict after several hours of consultation of guilty and fixed his term in the penitentiary at two years. When the prisoner heard the verdict he broke down and wept. His youth and bearing during the trial excited the sympathy of the bystanders.

Shooting Affair---Reports from Sevier County, Saturday has it that Thomas **Blair**, a former marshal of Maryville, became engaged in a quarrel about a seine, with a colored man in that county, and after a conflict of words the Negro, whose name could not be ascertained, pulled a pistol from his pocket. The pistol was fired two or three times and struck Blair twice.

Blair then went away from the scene of the shooting, obtained a shot-gun, hunted the Negro up and blew the whole top of his head off. The Negro died instantly. The reporter could not ascertain Blair's condition as reports conflicted, but think he will survive.

The following is the address of Rev. John **Silsby**, delivered at the funeral of Rev. D.M. **Wilson**, at Grandview, Rhea County, on Monday the 26th ult. [Sept. 26]

As the deceased had many friends in this county, we give it below.

Mr. Wilson was born March the 6th, 1819, at Charleston, N.H. In his 10th year the family removed to near Cincinnati, Ohio, where his father purchased a farm, and where the family continued to reside till the marriage of several of the senior members, among whom, besides the subject of this notice, are his elder brother, Theophilus, now a ruling Elder in the Avondale Presbyterian Church, and his sister, Mrs. M.J. **Pyle**, President of the Women's Presbyterial Home Missionary Society, of Cincinnati.

During his 20th year Mr. Wilson was a member of Woodward College, Cincinnati, while Drs. **Aydelott** and **Ray** were members of the faculty;

and from 1840 to 1844 he pursued his classical studies at Pleasant Hill Academy, before that institution became chartered as a college. He was graduated at Lane Theological Seminary in June, 1847, and was ordained the fall of that year at College Hill, Ohio, married the same day to Miss Emeline B. **Tomlinson** by Rev. Andrew **Benton**. Soon after they set sail for Syria as missionaries, under appointment of the American Board.

Mr. Wilson labored as a devoted missionary in that country till the spring of 1861, when the failing health of his wife compelled him to return to America. Upon his arrival in this country he took charge of the Congregational Church at New London, Butler County, Ohio, laboring there both as teacher and preacher till the winter of 1863-4, when he became connected with the Freedmen's Aid Society, with headquarters at Nashville. In 1864 he removed to Rodnor, Delaware County, Ohio, to labor as stated supply of the Presbyterian Church at that place, and remained there till 1867, when he removed to Athens, Tenn., to take charge of the Presbyterian Church. In the spring of 1884 he removed to Spring City, Tenn., to open work at various points along the C.S.R.R. In September of that year he took charge also of the Piney Falls Presbyterian Church at Grand View, Tenn., on the Cumberland plateau. The church was then without a house of worship, having held its services since its organization in 1876 in a temporary building. Through Mr. Wilson's efficient leadership, aided by our Board of Church Erection, the church now has a very neat and comfortable sanctuary, supplied with organ and other appointments for help in the services.

In the new cemetery just provided by this church, beautifully located on an eminence, a lot has been assigned, in accordance with his expressed preference, as his resting place. "Let me sleep," said he, "in the new Presbyterian Cemetery at Grand View till the resurrection morn."

The writer of the article in the Presbyterian Encyclopedia says, truthfully, of Mr. Wilson, "He is a man of extensive reading and varied information, and possesses a retentive and ready memory." No one can listen to his conversation without being surprised at his wide range of knowledge in history, theology and Biblical and general intelligence, and his wise discrimination in the use of the facts at his command.

The writer of this notice has known Mr. Wilson intimately since the spring of 1841, when we were both students at Cary's Academy. Always genial and pleasant in his social life, and enlivening conversation with apt quotations and spirited anecdote, he was indefatigable in his efforts for the spirited welfare of his fellow-students. He was the main stay of the students' prayer meeting at the academy, and of the weekly prayer meeting at father **McCary**'s, and to his faithfulness and that of a brother student, the late Rev. B.F. **Crary**, the writer attributes his own conversion.

Mr. Wilson seemed to be a man who was absolutely free from selfishness. Although uncompromising in his adhesion to principles, as fifty years given to leading reforms show, he never contended for mere personal interests. On the contrary he was always ready to sacrifice self when he could effect a good for another. The respectable and the despised, the esteemed and the outcasts were alike the objects of his benevolent efforts. Himself an indefatigable student, an acute thinker and able writer conversant with lofty themes of thought, he condescended to persons of the lowest intelligence, as well as to the despised and outcast in his efforts to do good, and shed light and to inspire minds with worthy hopes and desires. He was a reformer who built not on other men's foundations, but who always remembered that Christ came to save the lost.

His wife, and two children born in Syria, Mrs. Will A. **McTeer** and Rev. Prof. S.T. Wilson, of Maryville College, survive him.

Under The Waves---A rumor on the streets Monday to the effect that a boy was drowned in the **Kidd** pond, caused the *Times* reporter to hasten to the spot with haste. Jeremiah, son of Ben **Franklin**, had been hauling water, and he did not come back, a search was made which resulted in finding his body in three feet of water. Every effort possible was made to resuscitate the corpse and Dr. **Blankenship** came upon the scene and pronounced life extinct. Thomas **Lillard**, Esq., empanelled a jury, which resulted in a verdict of accidental drowning. Jeremiah was an inoffensive, hard working boy, and his untimely death causes universal regret.

Capt. S.M. **Rooker**, of Mooresville, Morgan Co. Indiana, came here Tuesday the 27th and remained two days. His father and mother were once citizens of Blount County. He called on Wesley **Norwood**, as he was one of the men who knew his father when he lived here.

Jeremiah **Franklin**, a young man, was drowned in a pond on the farm of David **Jones**. He was hauling water, took an epileptic spasm and fell in the water and drowned. He was a good boy and a hard worker.

Mrs. Jane **Gamble**, the mother of Mrs. James **Waters**, died at Knoxville, 2 o'clock Monday morning. Mrs. Gamble fell and hurt herself about two weeks ago. She was a woman eighty odd years old. She was buried at Walker's Chapel.

An infant child of Mr. & Mrs. A.G. **Howe**, of Knoxville, died on last

Friday. Dr. and Mrs. **Jennings** went to attend the funeral services.

Last week Mr. & Mrs. N.B. **Ellis** were summoned to Knox County by a telephone announcing that their daughter, Mrs. Ida **Roberts**, was not expected to live. Later, since writing the above, a letter to Charles Ellis says Mrs. Roberts' condition is improved and hopes are entertained of her recovery.

Mrs. Thomas **Ammons** departed this life at her home one mile east of Maryville on Tuesday, Sept. 27.

Married, at the residence of Mrs. **Gillespie**, on the 21st inst., by Rev. J.V. **Iddins**, Mr. J.M. **Harris** to Miss Jane **Holliday**, all of this county.

Wednesday, November 2, 1887

Obituary---Departed this life in Blount County, Oct. 27, 1887, James **Orr**, age 58 years. Again has death called from the checkered scenes of life a good man. Mr. Orr made a profession by a Godly walk and conversation until the day of his death. He knew and practiced nothing but honesty, truth and religion, he cherished no malice, he envied no man. His faith in the Christian religion was very strong and unwavering and supported him to the last, and at the time of his death was a member of the Methodist Church, South, although he cared but little about the name and creed of church relations, his hope was based alone on the sure, unshaken promises of God.

He worshiped at the altar of all denominations and often times as he thought of the far away home of the soul, his cup would overflow with joy and gladness, But, alas, he is gone, his feet now press the shining shore where no storm will ever beat on that beautiful strand.

Farewell dear wife and friends,
And kindred all around,
Prepare to meet me in that land
Where peace and joy will ever abound.

Brothers and sisters farewell,
Our union here must end,
But He who doeth all things well
Will bring you safe to your dear friend.

Dear children of my love,

104

I pray you think of me,
And in my footprints follow on,
And soon in Heaven you'll meet with me.

The wedding of Robert H. **Wallace** to Miss Mary **McCully**, on Wednesday, was the topic of special interest in the Tabor neighborhood last week. Prof. S.T. **Wilson** tied the knot in the presence of about thirty of the friends and relatives of the interested parties. A sumptuous dinner was served the company before the bride left the paternal roof to follow the fortunes of her husband. It goes without saying that the best of wishes of many friends go with the happy pair.

Died, on Saturday night, Oct. 29th, Mrs. John **Woodward**, of Nine Mile Creek, this county.

Mr. Ed. **Kidd** has been sick with lung and bilious trouble for about seven weeks. Mr. Kidd's usual weight is about 275 pounds, but his sickness has made a medium sized man of not more than 200 pounds.

Euphrasia **Hafley**, wife of A.C. Hafley, of the 12th District, who died on the 20th of September last, was born in this county in 1842, was and therefore in her 46th year. Her disease was flux; she was sick over two months. She left a husband and three children. She was a member of the M.E. Church since childhood. She was a daughter of William and Margaret **Goddard**. She died in the triumphs of living faith.

James **Orr**, near Louisville, died very suddenly on last Thursday, and his remains were interred at Duncan's Cemetery on last Saturday. Mr. Orr was a valued citizen of the county, and many friends regret his demise.

Nick **Russell**, of Long Hollow, sold his farm to a Knox County man, and will remove to Bradley County.

Miss Mary **Russell**, daughter of Nicholas Russell, of Long Hollow, is down with the malarial fever.

Mrs. Lucinda **Farr**, of Miller's Cove, fell one day last week and broke her arm.

Wednesday, November 9, 1887

The house of Mr. Ad. **Clemens**, with all its contents were burned Sunday night. Mr. Clemens lives on the Niles Ferry Road four and half miles from town.

Wednesday, September 5, 1888

Friendsville, September 3---An infant child of Lafayette **Jones**, of Clover Hill was brought to this place and buried yesterday. ---J.O. **Lee**.

Lay **Magill** was summoned to Monroe County, Saturday, by a telegram announcing the death of the brother-in-law, Millard **Hudson**. The telegram was received very late and the journey had to be made by private conveyance.

An Unwelcome Visitor---For several years the vicinity of Long Hollow has been harassed by wild beasts, and defamations have been committed which have at times caused the blood to run warm in the veins of the denizens. Persons traveling through this hollow at night---a very lonely road to travel---have been attacked, although such instances are not numerous. Several men have declared that they have seen a panther in that neighborhood, and one man ran a long distance to escape the deadly clutches of a very large panther.

An enormous one has recently been causing an upheaval in the neighborhood of Elkana **Johnson**, four miles from town. We are informed that upwards of thirty sheep have been destroyed, torn and mangled remains being found in several places. In order to ward off and frighten away the monster a large number of dogs were placed as guards over the sheep, but they, too, were found with their bodies severed in two. This voracious and wily beast has caused much anxiety in the neighborhood and vigils have been kept near sheep patches. But with all the watching the marauder still goes unpunished.

A posse of half a dozen men went out from Maryville Thursday morning, each armed with a rifle or shotgun. A days search was made, the woods scoured and bramble and briar patches ransacked, but no trace of the painter was seen. And it is probably very well that no encounter was had, for a panther is a terrible enemy to fight. Some of the men, however, are old hunters and would prove a match for, and probably silence the guns of the opposing force.

Old hunters inform us that panthers, wolves, etc., are constantly emigrating from one range of mountains to the other. They spend one month in the Smokies and inaugurate the next month in the Cumberlands with a big barbecue. A flock of sheep may be destroyed in a night by a roving panther or wolf, and by the time the sun rises next morning the guilty beast may be twenty miles away, hidden in the deep recesses and jungles of our giant mountains.

Campaign Of 1840---As far as we have been notified, the following are the names of men who voted for Harrison and Tyler in 1840. There are doubtless many more and we will leave this list standing in type for several weeks, and as fast as new names come in they will be appended: S.T. **Post**, William **Goddard**, David **Goddard**, R.L. **Hicks**, Richard **Nuchols**, Jo **Cumming**, J. **Johnson**, Elisha **Carpenter**, W.H. **Keeble**, A.A. **Kennedy**, Henry **McCulley**, Gilford **McReynolds**, J.D. **Parham**, J.E. **Cupp**, J.W. **Holt**, Newton **McConnell**, Clark **Blevins**, J.W. **Calvin**, Sylvester **Law**, Jacob **Nimon**, William J. **Hackney**, Wilson **Burchfield**, Elias **Davis**, Eli **Caylor**, Levi **Dunn**, J.N. **Emert**, William **Myers**, Daniel **Hedrick**, John **Currier**.

Wednesday, January 2, 1889

John Ed **Winters**, a clerk of long standing in G.A. **Toole**'s grocery store and a young man of energy and force of character, has changed his mode of living. On last evening he and Miss Celia A. **Gentry** were joined in the Holy bonds of wedlock. The *Times* wishes them a pleasant voyage o'er the placid sea of life.

Boys may think it fun to run out upon the streets at night, but after the experience of a few years they will wish their father had prevented them from doing so. Boys, take the advice of a man 64 years old and stay home of night with your good mother.

It is unknown to us who it is that occasionally makes night hideous with yells and unearthly screams. The persons who are guilty are the greatest sufferers, or if they are not now they will be in the future. It is well to inquire what has been the end of those in the past who were guilty of the same conduct.

Seigmund **Drick** died at Clover Hill on Saturday evening last, of hemorrhage of the lungs.

Mrs. Rogers, of Ellejoy, mother of Jesse **Rogers**, died last week.

Frank **Brooks** assaulted Will **Rankin** at Rockford on Christmas Day. Rankin resented the assault and struck Brooks with a gun, which is thought will result in his death.

A Good Man Gone---The sudden death of Dr. R. **Jennings** from heart trouble, Monday night, brought grief to his many friends. The doctor was feeling quite well at nine o'clock having been engaged with his wife in reading but remarked he would lay down, and in about five minutes Mrs. Jennings heard a little noise in the room to which he had retired and went in at once but one or two gasps was all and the work of life was closed. Dr. Jennings was one of the good men of Maryville. He came here about four years ago and had endeared himself to everybody who become acquainted with him. He had only a few weeks since moved into his nice residence on Indiana Street, and was prepared to spend the evening of life with his good wife nicely, joyously and in peace. But truly the Bible says, "In the midst of life we are in death." Services were held last evening at the residence of the deceased. Mr. & Mrs. A.G. **Howe**, son-in-law and daughter, of Knoxville, came down on the evening train. The remains of the doctor will be deposited in the cemetery at Knoxville. Peace will be his in a future world, as he is one of God's elect.

Wednesday, January 9, 1889

Friendsville---A new post office by the name of Cliff has been established at Big Springs, mail being supplied from the post office here.

Married, on Sunday, Dec. 30th, at the residence of H.H. **Jones**, Unitia, Mr. James C. **Beals** to Miss Nancy **Lee**, daughter of Ephriam Lee, living near town, S. **Mathews**, Esq., officiating. Mr. Beals is a brother of S.R. and L.H. Beals and his home is in Kansas. The bride is an estimable young lady and is loved and respected by all who know her. Her absence will be especially felt in the Sunday School and church where she is a constant worker. After the wedding the pair left for the home Mr. Beals' brother in Loudon County, from whence, on the following day, they left for their western home. ---J.O. Lee.

Jo **Edmondson** shot himself accidentally with a dynamite cartridge on Saturday, which leaves him less one thumb and two fingers on his right hand.

George **Kizer**, of Louisville, who was shot the night that Judge **Gibson** was to speak at that place, we are pleased to state is able to be about some. The *Times* sends congratulations to him that he is permitted to live with the good people still longer, and hoping that many years will still be his before he is called to a life beyond the river.

Hon. M.L. **McConnell**, whom the *Times* announced last week as dangerously sick, died on Thursday last. His funeral occurred on Friday. Mr. McConnell's health had been failing for some time. There was rather a complication of troubles which produced physical and mental paralysis, which resulted in his death. The deceased has been a prominent man and has filled several prominent official positions. He was a Captain in the 2nd Tennessee Cavalry during the late war. After the war he was in the House of Representatives, and afterwards in the Senate. From 1878 he was district attorney, his term expiring in 1886.

Wednesday, May 15, 1889

Shot Himself---George **James**, of the 5th District, accidentally shot himself in the bowels while fooling with his pistol, last Saturday night. He died on Sunday morning, at seven a.m. If people will fool with pistols and guns they will probably themselves suffer or cause others to suffer by their carelessness.

Dr. J.H. **Gillespie**, an able and experienced physician who spent his life in the county, and died at an advanced age a few years since, once said to the writer that there was not a healthier locality to be found anywhere in the country than Maryville. He had watched closely a long lifetime through a large practice; and, he said, there was an epidemic in about the year 1844, caused by a large mill dam on the western part of the town which confined the water until it became somewhat stagnant, and filled the town with a deadly fever, but when the dam was torn out, the fever disappeared, health was restored, and since that time there had been no place in the county, not even in the mountains with their pure, fresh and invigorating breezes, where there were fewer cases of sickness or deaths, in proportion to the number of inhabitants, than had been in Maryville. ---Will A. **McTeer**.

Gainesville, Georgia---A man named William C. **Wallace** died here a few days ago, who was born in Maryville Oct. 7th, 1827. He moved to Florida in time of the late war and had been living here nine years. He was injured by a railroad accident about a year ago, and had never recovered. Mr. Wallace was a very popular man in Gainesville. ---(part of a letter to the *Times* from R.S. **Phelps**.)

Large obituary of George Glenn **Cooper**, born Oct. 6, 1868 in Fair Haven, Ohio and died May 10, 1889 in Maryville, Tennessee. Attended

Maryville College.

Seaton---John **Waters**, living near Piney Level, died on Wednesday the 8th, Rev. P. **Henry** conducted the burial services. He had been sick for five weeks with scrofula. Leaves a wife and one child.

Aunt Sally **Walker**, of whom the *Times* spoke a few weeks since as having willed the M.E. Church a house and lot, is still quite feeble. She is seventy odd years old. ---Theodore **Rowan**.

Charles **Wilson** was in Maryville one day last week when he, for the first time in his life saw a railroad train. He was much excited when he saw it running.

Wednesday, June 5, 1889

The Colored People---Addie, son of Mr. & Mrs. Jackson **Hannum**, died last Wednesday morning, and was buried on the Methodist Hill Thursday afternoon. Addie was about 15 years of age. He had a very bright mind, and bade fair to be a great power in his race.

[Circuit Court Proceedings. Names mentioned are: Anthony **Scott**, J.C. **Finley**, Jane **Murr**, Mary **Simmerly**, Jacob **Simmerly**, Lime **Blevins**, Samuel **Dunlap**, George **McCully** and William **Snider**.]

George W. **Hutchinson** and Laura **Kidd** were married last Saturday night. Mr. Hutchinson is the man who is indicted for shooting at Miss Kidd's father, because he refused to give his consent to the marriage. It is not known now what shape the case will take since the marriage is consummated.

Bud [Anthony] **Scott**, who was charged and tried for obtaining fifty cents under false pretense from a woman here in town, was sent to the State prison for three years. Bud pays dearly for his fifty cents.

Wednesday, June 12, 1889

Letter written by R.S. **Phelps** from Gainesville, Georgia, June 3, 1889.

Died on the 24th, at the home of her husband at WaKeeney, Kansas, Mrs. M.K. **Brown**, wife of W.B. Brown, a graduate of Maryville College and son of Mrs. M.E. Brown of this vicinity, after a very brief illness in the 29th year of her age. By Tuesday's train Miss Ethal Brown, sister of the bereaved husband left for the home of her brother and would be joined at Knoxville by a sister of the deceased who would accompany her.

Died at her home three miles east of Maryville on the 10th inst., Mrs. Elizabeth **Cowan**, widow of late Sam F. Cowan, aged about 70 years and was interred in the Clark Graveyard yesterday. Funeral services by Prof. G.S.W. **Crawford**.

A child of Sam **McCammon** of the 6th District, died on Monday last.

Wednesday, June 19, 1889

Before the lynching of E.R. **Reynolds** and T.J. **Lloyd** at Huntsville, Scott County, Tenn., they were both given an opportunity to speak, which they embraced and confessed that they murdered Mrs. **Harness** and her son, and remarked we are ready to die.

Just now there is great interest manifested in the re-interment of the remains of ex-Governor John **Sevier**. And on that account old relics are hunted up. We have one now before us of a deed for a tract of land or lot in Maryville immediately opposite the *Times* office. The grant was to Samuel **Love** for the immense sum of twenty-five cents, paying for a whole quarter of an acre of land. The deed was executed on the 12th day of June, 1809 attested by the Secretary of State Robert **Huston**, whose home was in Blount County. The number of the grant was 530, showing that the grants made by the State had been but few. The deed is in possession of George A. **Toole** of this city.

Returned Home---Jacob **Henry**, the brawny, colored blacksmith, of Maryville, who some time since went to work at the Custom House as janitor, has gone home. He got enough of government pie. ---*Knoxville Journal*.

Charles **Parham** and Miss Nora **Hyden** were married at the home of Rev. D. **Hodsden** on last Thursday evening. The *Times* wishes them a long happy and prosperous life. The wedding was a surprise to many and yet many others were expecting it from their devotion to each other for a long time.

Robert **Martin** had sunstroke last Sunday. He was unconscious for a part of the day but has recovered somewhat from its effects.

111

James **Hall**, colored, received notice of a pension allowance amounting to $112.40. This will be a good start for James if he puts into a nice little farm.

Cam **Boyd**'s little daughter, six years old, wandered off from home last Sunday in the 8th District, which produced a sensation in the neighborhood. The neighborhood were all out hunting for her. She was found at Tobe **McConnell**'s.

L.H. **Beals**, of Friendsville, had a dog that became mad and bit some of his stock and they became mad. The dog and stock were all killed. Some other stock that was bitten by the same dog has not yet exhibited any signs of hydrophobia.

It is said the *Times* failed to notice the death of Aunt Sallie **Walker** some two weeks since, who lived some three miles southeast of Maryville. She was a Christian woman with noble asperation, and her intimate friends have no doubt as to her now occupying a mansion in the Promised Land.

Uncle Jerry **Hudson** was out on Washington Street last Monday. He walked with a cane.

[T.J.] **Lloyd** and [E.R.] **Reynolds**, the Helenwood, Tenn., murderers were taken from jail on the night of the 11th and 12th inst., and hanged on a tree near the jail.

Wednesday, June 26, 1889

Letter written by John H. **Morton** from La Veta, Colorado.

Marriage---Married at the residence of the bride's mother, Miss Erie **Brown** to Mr. M.M. **Rankin**, on the evening of June 19th at half past seven o'clock.
Prof. S.T. **Wilson** performed a neat and impressive ceremony in the presence of a small number of the relatives of the contracting parties.
After congratulations and good wishes, the company repaired to the dining room where June's choicest flowers decked a well arranged table, loaded with good things.
The evening was spent very pleasantly and it was concluded that the news had not got out and that the boys and the bells were all quiet, when suddenly a sound arose, and hackmen put on brakes and grasped the lines

tighter, the Prof. turned pale with concern for his horse and carriage, the bridegroom with his ready thought pulled down the window curtain to protect his bride, the stoutest held their breath and waited for the worst. But in a moment the noise ceased and a well-known laugh was heard and it was soon discovered that three of the company had attempted to serenade with two tin pans and a horn.

Mr. & Mrs. Rankin accompanied by Mr. J.G. **Newman** and Miss Ida **Alexander** go to Mount Horeb to visit before bidding Maryville goodbye for their school in Huntsville. ---J.I. **McIlvaine**.

The Rockford Tragedy---Quite an excitement amongst the colored people on Friday last was caused by the killing of William **Woods** by Bill **Johnson**. So far as anybody knew they had been friends up to the time of the tragedy. It is said they had on a few occasions been practicing what is called tragedy on the stage---sham fights, and it is said Johnson would occasionally get so excited that he had once or twice came near doing what he finally did at Rockford on last Friday. On that occasion the matter commenced with a joke but ended in the one killing the other. Johnson first struck Woods with a stone, felling him, but Woods arose and started for Johnson with shovel in hands when Johnson drew his knife and plunged it into the left breast of Woods which ended his life in about five minutes.

Johnson started for Maryville to give himself up, and remarked, "this will hang me."

Sheriff **Armstrong** was telephoned and Deputy **Blankenship** and W.A. **Coker** left for the scene of murder, but met Johnson on the way and took possession of him and brought him into town.

The Coroner John **Currier** was notified, who summoned a jury to hold an inquest which after the examination of witnesses returned the following:

State of Tennessee, Blount County. An inquisition held at Maryville in the County and State aforesaid on the 21st day of June, 1889, before John M. Currier, coroner of said county, upon the body of William Woods there lying dead by jurors whose names are hereto subscribed who upon their oaths do say that the said deceased William Woods came to his death by a stab in the left side with a knife inflicted by J.W. Johnson and the jurors further finds that the killing was felonious. Given under our hands this the 21st day of June, 1889: J.D. **Moore**, J.W. **Culton**, Jacob **Henry**, Sam P. **Rowan**, Harry **Barger**, J.E. **Patterson**, F.D. **Fulkerson**, John M. Currier, Coroner.

Died---Mrs. Ida F. **Harper** (formerly **Hurly**) on the 18th inst., at

Springtown, Texas. Many old friends remember Miss Ida Hurly.

Look out for mad dogs. A number of these vicious animals have been in and about Louisville and Misers. James **Prater** was bitten by one last Friday. One cow was bitten and went mad.

John **McPeters** hung himself on Sunday at Tipton's Station. No cause known. Later: The cause of the hanging was a difficulty between himself and wife. Mr. McPeters did not accomplish much as he was cut down before death, and he still lives for another trial of life.

Elcana **Johnson**, an old citizen of the 9th District, died on Monday last.

Wednesday, July 3, 1889

The Colored People---Lida, infant daughter of Mr. & Mrs. Henry **Ambrister**, died last Saturday morning. She was buried Sabbath afternoon. The bereaved family has our deepest sympathies.

Died, at his home in Baker's Creek, May the 21st, Peeler **Chapman**, son of Robert and Sarah Chapman. Age, sixteen years.

The M.E. Quarterly meeting was held with the church at Pleasant Hill. The little son of Presiding Elder **Petty**, two or three years old, died on Thursday at his home in Morristown, which prevented the Elder from being present.

Rev. D. **Bowles** and Mrs. Jesse **Stanley** done some good religious services with the convicts in the Maryville jail last Sunday week at 3 p.m. But the last preaching came from William **Johnson** behind the iron grates, taking for his text on the decree of God the maxim, What is to be will be, and what ain't to be might happen. He did not define his text very closely, he did not say whether the killing of Bill **Woods** belonged to the would be's or might happen's. ---J. Stanley.

John **Huffstetler** and Miss Florence **Henry** were married Thursday evening. This teaching girls how to cut and make dresses does have such effects in this country. The *Times* wishes them long life, peace and prosperity.

Letter written by R.S. **Phelps** from Gainesville, Georgia.

Wednesday, July 10, 1889

Friendsville---Miss Jay **Hammer** is in Tuckaleechee Cove attending her grandfather, Lorenzo **Perkins**, who is very old and is not expected to live.

Mr. Luna A. **Moore** who lives near here and Miss Lou **McConnell**, of Loudon County, were married by Esq. **Greer** at his residence last evening. ---J.O. **Lee**.

A Sad Loss---John Franklin **Magill** died at his parent's residence on July 5, at 4:30 a.m. He was the son of J.M. and M.E. Magill, and was born in Monroe County, where, as well as in Blount County, a large number of relatives mourn his early departure.

Frank graduated from Maryville College at the recent commencement, though unable to be present to receive his diploma. More than three months ago he was injured while playing ball, and since then has endured untold agony. His wide circle of acquaintances in college and in the vicinity have watched his battle with disease with the solicitude, for few young men have been more generally beloved. But, just on the threshold of post-collegiate life, he was smitten down by the dread destroyer.

The large assembly gathered in the college chapel on last Saturday morning testified to the general esteem in which he was held. The chapel was draped with the insignia of grief and the casket was covered with floral offerings. The very solemn funeral services were conducted by Prof. **Crawford** and participated in by Rev. Messrs. **Bassett, McNeal, McConnell** and Prof. **Wilson**. The interment was in the College Cemetery.

Frank was a humble, conscientious Christian. He was converted under the ministry of Rev. D. **McDonald** in 1881, and united with the Presbyterian Church at Madisonville where his membership remained. Soon after his conversion he decided to become a minister, and came to Maryville to prosecute his studies toward that end. Here he was an honest and earnest student and steadily developed in mental and moral power. His best year was his last one. His Christian faith and zeal have been manifest during his entire illness. He is at rest.

Mrs. Martha **Logan**, of the 6th District, died on last Saturday morning.

A child of Daniel **Hedrick** of the 8th District, died on Monday and was buried at Piney Level.

Calvin **Coulter** who lived on Crooked Creek, died Tuesday morning at three o'clock, with pneumonia. He will be buried at Piney Level.

Wednesday, July 17, 1889

W.H. **Lawson** who has been living in Indiana for a number of years has returned here and purchased the farm owned by Charles **Boyd**, east of Maryville.

George **Davis** received a pension as a fireman on the Ratler during the war for injury to a foot. He was granted a pension of $2 per month from November 1883 and $4 per month from March 27th, 1889.

Mrs. Nancy Jane **Duggan**, wife of J.W. Duggan, our County Superintendent of public schools, died on Wednesday the 10th inst., of catarrhal fever, aged 28 years. Mrs. Duggan leaves six children, the youngest of which is nineteen months old.

Wednesday, July 24, 1889

Letter written by R.S. **Phelps** from Gainesville, Georgia.

Painful Accident---Isaac S. **Russell**, of Crooked Creek, met with a bad accident on last Friday. He was moving a threshing machine and riding on it at the time, and on account of the road his wagon was about to upset and he jumped to clear himself when his foot was caught by the brake lever of the machine which threw him several feet upon his head which striking some slick stone, lifted the scalp off one side of his head from the forehead past the crown. Dr. **Robbins** was called in and set the scalp.

Alex **Henry** (colored) and his wife who live in Knoxville, are in trouble. Alex married a young woman and is now jealous of her as most old men get to be who marry young girls.

Mrs. **Swim** of this place, died on last Saturday evening at 5 o'clock. Her remains were sent to Grainger County for interment. Her disease was cancer.

Rev. R.L. **Jenkins** will preach the funeral sermon of Mrs. Martha J. **Whitehead** on next Sunday the 28th, at Six Mile Church.

A man by the name of **Frye** was arrested and put in jail on the charge of stealing Luke **Calloway**'s horse down on the Little Tennessee.

116

John **Thomas**, brother of A.J. Thomas has just returned to his old home of thirty-two years ago. Mr. Thomas will remain during the summer.

A year and a half old filly belonging to T.C. **Clark**, hung herself Thursday night by slipping her head and neck into a crack of the barn. She was dead next morning.

Wednesday, July 31, 1889

The man who hired the horse of **Edmondson, McKenzie** & Co., has been found, arrested and turned into the Blount County jail to await the action of the Circuit Court. His name is **Ross** and is a native of Roane County, but was traveling for a silverware firm. It is said he also hired a horse at Mossy Creek and took it to Athens where he was captured and turned over to Blount County.

John **Tally**, of Tipton's Station, died of typhoid fever last Wednesday night. Mr. Tally has been connected for some time with the K. & A. Railroad.

Died---At Jockcy, Greene County, Tenn., on July 21st, 1889, Mr. W.F. **Reser**, aged 73 years. Deceased was the father of Mrs. J.T. **Anderson**, Mrs. J.M. **Allen** and Mrs. B.C. **Seehorn** of this county.

Frye, the young man charged with stealing Luke **Calloway**'s horse, had a preliminary trial set for Monday, 1 p.m., at which time he waived examination and goes to jail and awaits the action of the grand jury.

Hawk Day---Was it a good day for hawks? Mr. Lafayette **Everett** on the 22nd inst., shot with a rifle six large, blue hawks at the foot of the mountain near Melrose Springs, went out after 12 p.m. and got home by 5 p.m. with the result above stated. This beats the past record as far as heard from. The writer saw the birds and procured one tail for a fan. Reference: Wallace **Milsap**, William **Henry**, J.S. **Bonham**.

Wednesday, August 7, 1889

Eusebia---George **Norton**, an industrious farmer and brother of J.G. Norton, Esq., fell from his barn loft and broke his left arm near the shoulder.

W.H. **Drake**, assisting in sawing a log, was thrown about 14 feet high by a prize pole. He fell among some brush and is pretty badly shaken up. ---J.W. **Duggan**.

A Shooting---Bill **Gregory** went to the house of Alvin **Smith** in Happy Valley Saturday night, and stoned the house. Smith took his gun and went out in the road to look for the one who was doing that work, when Gregory arose from behind a clump of weeds and shot him, six or eight shot hitting him on the head. Smith attempted to shoot Gregory while running but his gun cap failed to make fire. Gregory has not been arrested that we know of.

The little child of William **Goddard**, of Knoxville, who had been sent here hoping to save its life, died on last Thursday and was buried Friday. Rev. D. **Hodsden** officiating at the funeral services.

The father of Dr. **Bond** was to some extent prostrated by heat and has been in bed for a week or so. He is ninety-three years old.

George **Norton**, of the 13th District fell from his barn loft last Wednesday, breaking his collar-bone. He has good chances of recovering.

Martha J. **Cupp** of the 8th District, died yesterday morning at her home of malarial fever, aged 14 years.

Andy **Waters** of the 18th District, died at his home on Saturday last.

Mrs. Ruthe **Lee**, wife of T.R. Lee, of Friendsville, died of consumption at her home on the 23rd of July. Rev. David **Bowles** officiated at the funeral services.

James **Hannum** was arrested on Saturday night by Sheriff **Armstrong**, on a writ issued against him on a charge of the violation of the person of Lilly Ann **Peterson**, a girl of ten years old. A preliminary hearing was set for today.

Wednesday, August 14, 1889

Albert **Coning**, and Miss Martha **Thomas**, were married in Virginia on the 5th of August. They came here and visited Albert's father and family. They will make their home in Knoxville.

Cam **Hutton**, of Miser has been dangerously sick for some time, he had been afflicted with paralysis, which will probably terminate in his death. Information last Saturday said he could not live.

Rebecca **McCoy**, a sister to Cal McCoy, died on last Wednesday. She was 80 years old.

A Demorest medal contest was held at Middle Settlements. Miss Cora **Anderson** received the silver medal.

Missing---Kingston, Tenn., August 9, 1889. Mr. J.W. **Bowman**. **Lipman** a peddler, is missing and any information obtained about him will be greatly appreciated by his wife and child. It is feared that he has been foully dealt with. ---B. **Shepera**.

Wednesday, August 21, 1889

Letter written by R.L. **Phelps** from Gainesville, Georgia.

Friendsville, August 19---Joseph **Peters** eldest son of Jacob Peters, is lying dangerously ill from typhoid fever at the home of his father near town.

Mrs. Rhoda **Mahoney** of Miser is confined to he bed from cancer ulcers having appeared over the entire breast; about a year ago she had an operation performed on her but it failed to effect a cure.

James H. **Sexton** and family arrived last week from Iowa. Mr. Sexton is a native of Tennessee but emigrated some years ago to the west; his health failing he returns to recuperate. ---J.O. **Lee**.

Three cows belonging to Riley **Lee**, died from being bitten by a mad dog. Some other parties in the Friendsville vicinity have also lost cattle in the same way.

John **Wear** was arrested one night last week, on an affidavit of Mrs. **Woods**. John had been taking a little too much red liquor and felt in a living mood and so went to see Mrs. Wood, who is a widow. When John told her who he was, she screamed and would not be reconciled, so John was taken with a leaving. John says women, wine and whiskey shall not get him into anymore trouble. John gave bond for his appearance.

Samuel **McNally** of the 13th District, died at his home of paralysis.

At Pleasant Grove, Rev. R. **Coulter** preached last Sabbath, when it was observed that there were 32 persons whose name was Coulter.

At a wedding at Stephen **Graves** of the 13th District on Saturday night there was a fight gotten up between **Tipton** and **Baily**. Arch **Farmer** undertook to interfere when he was cut with a knife in the breast, back, shoulder, and thumb, and was struck with a rock on the bridge of the nose. He is regarded as being in a dangerous condition. Some of the persons who were in thr fight had been indulging in that good article, which always gets up trouble and fights. The *Times* knows of no arrests being made.

Prof. W.P. **Hastings**, who had lost a young horse in the mountains came in to advertise him. We had the matter ready to strike off when the horse came home. It must have known that if it was advertised, in the *Times* it would have to come home, so it came home to save making it a public matter.

Rev. William **Wetherald**, of Toronto, Canada, who is doing work in connection with the Friends' Church in the United States, occupied the pulpit at Hickory Grove last Sunday morning and at Maryville at night. He is a vigorous man to be near three-score years and ten in age. He left on Monday morning for Ohio.

John E. **Shedden** was in Maryville, on business last Monday. He says the new railroad split his farm in two. The Co., makes him a plank fence half mile long, for right of way.

From dispatches in the paper it appears that Mr. William **Thaw**, a prominent and worthy citizen of Pittsburg, died a few days ago in Paris. Mr. Thaw was a warm friend of the Maryville College and had contributed large amounts of money in its behalf.

Sam S. **Henry** had a horse bitten by a mad dog in the 14th District. The horse died.

Miss Phebe J. **Cowan** died on Sunday night of consumption, age forty years.

Maurice **Hyden**, who came home from Knoxville sick, some four weeks since still lies in bed with a slight malarial fever.

Wednesday. August 28, 1889

Funeral Services---I will preach the funeral sermon of Sister Jane **Johnson** at Louisville, Tenn., on the 2nd Sunday in September at 3 p.m. ---D.S. **Hodsden**.

Drowned---John **Tullock**, who was in Maryville last Thursday with his team and wagon, left for home taking out some goods for his store in the 7th District, and drove into Six Mile Creek after the heavy rain. The creek was up so high that the water ran over his wagon and drowned one of his mules, the other one was loosened from the wagon and saved. The wagon and the goods went on down stream. The *Times* has not heard whether they were recovered or not.

Mr. **Hockenjos**, one of the injured ones in the Cumberland Gas wreck last week, died on Sunday.

Franklin and wife who were in jail, left last Saturday night for parts unknown. Time not out by three weeks.

William **Walker** brought into the *Times* office a nail made by John **Hess** 89 years ago.

Rumor has it that the time of the wedding of James **Carnes**, of Knoxville, and Miss Della **Allen** of this place, will be next Tuesday morning, leaving for Knoxville and house keeping on the morning train.

Captain **Freshour** brought two more moonshiners into Maryville last week. The mountains in Monroe County are full of them. Whisky in Monroe is used in the place of milk. Wormy chestnuts makes the richest kind of whisky juice.

The schoolhouse at Clover Hill was burned one night last week. It was evidently the work of an incendiary. There had been no fire in or about the building, and when discovered, it was breaking through the roof. Mr. Will **Cochran** was teaching in the house.

Mr. **Dilge**, of North Carolina, was at James **Everett**'s last week on his way to Indiana. He lived a neighbor to Mrs. **Boston**, who is 121 years old. Mrs. Boston has only weighed 52 pounds for 20 years. She was one of the two surviving pensioners. She died last week.

121

Married---On the evening of the 21st, 1889, Mr. E.B. **Mason** and Miss Anna **Moore**. Everybody was expecting this marriage but its suddenness took all by surprise. On Wednesday evening, after a change of program for the future was agreed upon, they took a buggy ride, and stopped at Dr. **Bartlett**'s a few minutes. The beauty of home life and novelty of keeping house so attracted them at the home of Mrs. Bartlett that they had the Doctor perform the ceremony and they went away believing they were really married, and the *Times* believes so too, as the record in Clerk **Cunningham**'s office, gives evidence of the same. The wedding will be just as good as if they had made two or three hundred dollar spread of money over it. The happy couple left for Johnson City on Thursday morning train where they will remain for a short time, after which Mr. Mason will begin the work of his life, preaching the unreachable riches of Christ.

Mad Dogs---Let everybody look to the condition of their dogs, as there are mad dogs all over the country. A young man shot one in Maryville the other day. All worthless dogs had better be slain. Your pet dog may bite your children or your neighbor's children more readily than some old worthless dog. Attend to this matter at once.

Wednesday, September 4, 1889

No Charges Made---We your committee appointed by D.S. **Hodsden**, the pastor of the Maryville circuit M.E. Church, to investigate the rumors against the moral character of Ben C. **Taylor**, an exhorter in said church, find after a thorough and impartial investigation of the case that there are no grounds for any charge to be brought against the said Ben C. Taylor, and we further find no just grounds for such rumors: Elisha **Carpenter**, J.A. **Goddard**, W.T. **Barnhill**. September 3rd, 1889. I concur in the above statement, D.S. Hodsden, pastor.

Letter written by J.C. **Tullock** from Rosendale, Missouri.

Friendsville, September 2---Joe **Peters**, who was mentioned in my last letter as sick with typhoid fever is better.

Joseph **Beals**, an old and highly respected citizen living near Unitia is not expected to live. He is the father of L.H. Beals of this place.

Miss Della **Allen**, a former typo of this office, was married on last Monday morning to Mr. James **Carnes** of Knoxville. They left on the morning train for their home in Knoxville. May peace and success crown their lives.

Rev. W.E. **Ijams** will return to Maryville. He wrote here to engage rooms for a home. In a private letter to the *Times*, he said "I find no place that suits me better than Maryville." The people here will give him a hearty welcome.

A family by the name of **Nickerson** from near Fountain City, Indiana, came in last evening. Their object is to make this country their home. They are farmers.

David **Alexander**, a young man of 22 years, died the 29th ult., [August] at his home near Unitia, in Loudon County, of malarial fever.

Mrs. Isaac **Russell** died of consumption in the 8th District last Saturday.

A child of Will **Everett** died last evening.

Mrs. Charles **Gentry** fell off the Pistol Creek foot log last Saturday and was badly injured in her left side.

Fred **Spangler**, died at the residence of P.T. **Haggard**, at 2:30 o'clock, Friday of typhoid fever, was buried at the Lutheran Church 7 miles southeast of Knoxville Saturday evening.

Nathan **Wilson** who came here from Indiana some three years since, on account of very poor health, died yesterday morning at 4 o'clock. His wife had gone north and was absent at the time of his death.

Wednesday, September 11, 1889

Mr. **Yearout** who has been living near D.W. **Trotter**, had his leg broken a few days ago. He is an old man but it was thought unnecessary to take his leg off.

A new post office has been granted, and is to be called Hebronville. It is located between Gambell and Ellejoy, John M. **Waters** is appointed postmaster.

Thomas **Cannon**, who is reported to have killed **Hammontree** in Loudon County, was arrested in Texas and is now in the Loudon County

Jail.

Mrs. James **Walker**, who lived on Nine Mile, died last Sunday morning.

John **Davis**, of the 14th District, died last Friday night of lung trouble.

Wednesday, September 18, 1889

Colored People---George **McSwain**, of North Carolina, a blacksmith for Hastings & Moore, died last Saturday night at Jacob **Henry**'s. He was sick only eight days. McSwain leaves a wife to mourn his loss. She has our deepest sympathies.

The family of John **McCullock**, deceased, will remove to Dunbar, Nebraska this week. The family has lived here a great many years and was highly respected. The *Times* sends its good regards with them.

Miss Mattie **Raines**, a young lady of 22 years, died at her father's home in this city last Thursday morning of fever. She was only sick one week. She was buried at Piney Level.

The memorial sermon of the late Fred **Spangler** was preached at the Baptist Church last Sabbath, by Rev. **Smith**. The audience was large and attentive.

Her Head Is Level---A Democrat who marries a Republican girl should always provide her with a good Republican paper, like the *Maryville Times*, if he wants his children raised up right. It's nonsense to talk about a mother raising her children in the way they ought to go, on what they get out of a Democrat paper. A young, Republican mother sent in and subscribed for the *Times*, the other day. She said she could not live and do right on reading a Democrat paper.

Wednesday, September 25, 1889

The broom factory of P.T. **Haggard** burned on the night of the 18th. (continued)

Friendsville, September 23---Your correspondent paid a visit yesterday to Mrs. Sarah **Ellis**, who has lived under all the administrations of the government and is one of the oldest, if not the oldest, person living in the county. She was born in Orange County, North Carolina, on the 15th of December 1794, and was brought here by her parents in 1799, three years after the State's admission, and only eight years after Knoxville was laid out as a town. Her parents first settled on Cloyd's Creek, but afterwards removed to a farm about one-half mile from present residence, which is one mile east of town. Although near 96 years of her age her senses are but little impaired, and her physical preservation is something remarkable. I was shown a quilt top, which in work and arrangement was almost perfect, that was pieced by her in her ninetieth year. She also pieced five squares of a quilt in her ninetieth year, besides samples of her work of that kind given to her friends as souvenirs. During the present season she peeled and dried with her own hands a considerable quantity of fruit, which I found to be excellent in quality. Her age and good recollection has made her an object of interest to all, and her accounts of the customs and habits of life of the early settlers are very interesting. In her girlhood days Mrs. Ellis enjoyed uninterrupted good health, when a cancerous growth appeared on her eyebrow which became so malignant as to destroy the sight of one eye. Had it not been for this, there is hardly a doubt but that she would complete her century of existence. Longevity is inherent in her family, her father dying at the age of 74 and her mother at 90. Of her 11 brothers and sisters, all reached middle life and 4 of the number living to be between 80 and 90 at time of death. Six children were born to her, our jolly fellow-townsman, W. Rufus **Jones** and Mrs. David **Poland** being of the number. ---J.O. **Lee**.

Maryville College---Mr. William **Thaw** of Pittsburg, Pa., on of the most liberal benefactors the college has ever had, died at Paris, France, Aug. 17th, 1889. He bequeathed $5,000 to the college at his death. His bequests to the college, since he began to aid it, amount to over $60,000.

The German Baptist or brethren will have a communion service on the third Sunday and Saturday in October, at their church at Oakland, six miles southwest of here on the Niles Ferry Road.

Mrs. Stone, wife of Samuel **Stone**, died on the 17th inst. Mr. Stone lives just outside of Blount County.

The old Missionary Baptist Church in Millers Cove has been weather boarded and re-roofed. The nails used in the old building were hand made and the building is said to be 100 years old, built out of poplar and pine logs, hewed. We get these facts from Samuel **Hatcher**.

Wednesday, October 2, 1889

Wedding---Cards are out for the marriage of Miss Lula **Cates**, of Maryville, and Mr. Will A. **Knabe**, of Knoxville, on Wednesday the 9th day of this month, at the M.E. Church, South, at half-past seven p.m. The *Times* is pleased to make this announcement, and commend the parties for making the contract for a partnership for life, trusting and believing they will have smooth sailing out on the great ocean of time, and that long life and happiness will be theirs.

G.B. **Delzell** and John Delzell, of West Liberty, Ill., have been visiting old friends in Blount. The former left here 39 years ago, says he would have not known Maryville if he had been unloaded in the town without being told what place it was. They left for their home this morning.

Lize **Boyd**, a colored woman died at Cloyd's Creek yesterday morning. She was alone when she died.

In the case of Walter **Dunn**, charged with horse stealing, he was found guilty and sentenced to seven years in the State Prison.

Wednesday, October 9, 1889

Goes For Life---The State vs. **Johnson**: In this case for murder, the jury found him guilty as charged in the indictment, but they said murder in the first degree with some mitigating circumstances. The point referred to as being in his favor was after he had knocked **Woods** down with a stone, Woods got up with a shovel in hand and went for him and struck at him when Johnson drew his knife and plunged it into him which was a death cut. The colored people were considerably excited over the case, so much so that it is believed by many, that a colored jury would not have said, with mitigating circumstances.

The White Caps are after the Mormons in this State, and the old rascals skipped. It is well they did as they would have been handled pretty roughly if caught.

Coker Creek Gold---We are glad to meet at our office Monday last, I.T. **Tate**, Esq., of the Coker Creek gold regions in Monroe County. He brought down with him and sent to the United States mint at Philadelphia, through the First National Bank of Athens, 117 ½ penny-weights of gold dust. This dust coins 92 ½ cents to the penny-weight, and is current in the mining region at 90 cents. 'Squire Tate's largest export of gold at one time from Coker Creek was 800 penny weight---some five or six years ago.

A Chicago company, headed by I.C. **Gifford**, of the board of that city, is actively at work preparatory to the development of the Coker Creek mines. They have erected three buildings, including the assay office. Their purpose is to put up a quartz mill from ten to twenty stamp capacity. Their works are now at what is known as Whip-Poor-Will mines, and the active operation of these will begin at once. In fact ores are now being taken from a vein twenty-four inches in thickness, specimens being of good paying character.

Mr. Isaac Tate, the father of our friend, has lived in this section of which we write more than fifty years, and in that time has seen enough gold taken out to almost pay the debt of Tennessee and build the Knoxville Southern by Athens, too. He is still in good health and expects to see Coker Creek become as famous as California did in 1849. --- *Atlanta Post.*

Og **Henry**, who was a slave of James Henry, was in town last Monday. He is of the opinion that he is one hundred years old. The old man lives with John Henry, a son of James Henry, of Brick Mill.

A letter from Miss Maggie **McCulloch**, a few days since, reveals the fact that they arrived safely at Dunbar, Nebraska and, were well, and were well pleased with the outlook. Mrs. McCulloch, stood the trip quite well, and was rested up when the letter was written.

A colored boy by the name of Wal **Barger** who was arrested some time since with other boys in stealing, but the cases were compromised and turned out, was indicted by the Grand Jury last week for stealing a bag of shot out of the depot since the compromise. On trial was found guilty and sent to the work house for six months.

Yesterday morning we had our first frost. It was one that was seen, and the chill it produced made us think of winter, warm clothes and good fires.

Wednesday, October 16, 1889

Reward---Horace **Shedden**, apprenticed to me by the County Court of Blount County, run away from me Sept. 9, 1889 and has not been heard of since. A reward of 6 ½ cents and no thanks will be given anyone returning him to me. ---John E. Shedden, Oct. 14, 1889.

The Wedding---Announced in the *Times* two weeks since, Miss Lula **Cates** was married on Wednesday, the 9th day inst., to Mr. Will **Knabe**, of Knoxville. The occasion was one of great interest. A number of Mr. Knabe's friends came over from Knoxville. The church was beautifully decorated and literally packed with men, women and children. Rev. W.D. **Akers** officiated, using the solemn marriage ritual laid down by his church. The happy couple left for their home in Knoxville Thursday morning. Our kindest regards go with them.

Letter written by R.L. **Phelps** from Blountsville, Alabama.

Married, at the residence of the bride's parents, Mr. & Mrs. Silas **Huddleston**, of Dublin, Ind., Oct. 9th, 1889, Charles R. **Hill**, of Maryville, Tenn., to Miss Rosetta Huddleston, Rev. William **West** officiating. There were present two brothers of the bride, Dr. H.P. Huddleston, of Maryville, Tenn., and Dr. A.F. Huddleston and family, of Winchester, Ind., her uncle, Aquilla **Binford** and wife, of Thorntown, Ind., and aunt Eliza **Pickett**, of Montgomery County, Indiana, also Miss Anna **Newby**, of Maryville, Tenn., and a few relatives and friends of Dublin. After the ceremony all partook of a splendid supper. Many handsome and appropriate presents were received. In a few days Mr. & Mrs. Hill will go on a visit to relatives in Ohio, after which they will start to Maryville, their future home.   ---*Wayne Register.*

In the case of the State vs. James **Hannum**, after a tedious trial of two days he was found guilty by a jury of twelve men, and sentenced to the State Prison for twenty-five years. A new trial was asked, which was overruled by the court, and an appeal taken to the Supreme Court. On the report of the Grand Jury and by an affidavit of the sheriff, the jail was shown to be unsafe and the judge ordered a transfer to Knox County. To which point Hannum was conveyed Saturday morning, where he will remain till the case is reviewed on error assigned by the defense.

Wednesday, October 23, 1889

Letter written by R.L. **Phelps** from Blountsville, Alabama.

Maryville College---Prof. **Crawford** was called away last Monday to attend the funeral of Mr. William **Hart**, who died on Sunday at his home four miles north of Maryville. The deceased was for some time a student of Maryville College. His death is a source of great regret to all the students who knew him.

Mrs. Fayette **Everett**, of the 14th District, died last Friday, of consumption.

Jesse **Millsap**, a man about eighty year old living in the 14th District is very dangerously sick with dropsy.

William, son of Thomas **Hart**, of the Ninth District, died Sunday afternoon, of consumption and pneumonia.

Mrs. Nancy **McClain**, wife of John McClain, of the 12th District, died of consumption, last Saturday.

Mrs. William **Goddard**, is dangerously sick at her old home in the 12th District.

A daughter of Samuel **Keeble**, was married to a Mr. [Tilford] **Reagan**, last week, when a serenading party under the leadership of Cars **Breeden** and William **Barbary**, with guns, horns, etc., marched around the house cutting up some pranks like serenaders do when Mr. Keeble became excited and there was a little shoving and loud talk, especially after they broke a large jar for Mrs. Keeble and pushed the door down.

Wednesday, October 30, 1889

Letter written by R.L. **Phelps** from Blountsville, Alabama, October 25, 1889.

Five brothers named **Barnard** are to be hung in Hancock County on the 23rd of December next, for the murder of Henry **Sutton**.

The grain house of George C. **Davis**, in the 13th District was burned one night last week which contained 100 bushels of wheat and about the same amount of oats. It is not known how it caught on fire.

Henry **Russell**, an old man of 80 years, died of old age last Friday.

Rev. J.A. **Ruble** will preach the funeral sermon of Mrs. Laura **Hutchens**, daughter of Mr. Perry **Kidd**, at Mount Moriah, Wednesday, Nov. 6th at 10:30 a.m.

Married---On Wednesday last by Rev. M.A. **Hunt**, at his residence, Mr. James **Rule** and Miss Lizzie **Hanna**, of this place. Mr. Rule and wife will reside in northeast Maryville. The *Times* wishes them success through life.

Willie **Henry**, son of George Henry, of the 12th District, died on Monday last. Age 16 years.

A new post office has been established five and a half miles south of here. The office is named Block House and William **James** is appointed postmaster. It is to be on the Montvale route. The mail will pass out the road past Mr. **Broady**'s from Block House via Corn to Montvale. The office will be in the store of William James.

Wednesday, November 6, 1889

Mrs. **Sharp**, daughter of Andrew **Pitner**, died last Friday night, and was buried at Eusebia Cemetery on Sunday.

Mr. **Overman**, who went to Kansas a short time ago, was brought back from that State badly hurt, Monday evening. We have not the particulars.

Wednesday, November 13, 1889

The Colored People---Mr. Isaac **West**, a student of F.N. Institute, was called home on account of the illness of his father. He did not reach home in time to see his father alive. Isaac has returned to his studies and he has our deepest sympathies.

Daring Robbery---One of the boldest robberies ever committed in Maryville took place Monday morning about 11 o'clock, at the residence of John **Blankenship** on Washington Street. Mrs. Blankenship had gone across the street for a few minutes to the residence of Howard **Tedford**. During her absence a thief, stranger here, entered the house.
Mrs. Blankenship on returning home met him at the door. He inquired if Mrs. -----lived here and said that he had a note for her. Mrs. Blankenship told him there was no such person living in the neighborhood. He then left, going over the hill towards the Maryville City Mills. Mrs. Blankenship suspicion that he had been stealing something and entering the house found that some money and jewelry

including a fine scarf pin, the whole amounting to about twelve dollars, were missing. She at once sent word to her husband who is Deputy Sheriff, and he with Sheriff **Armstrong** and Constable **Coker** commenced hunting for the burglar. One man was suspicion on Monday afternoon but Mrs. Blankenship could not identify him as the one. Deputy Sheriff Blankenship went to Knoxville yesterday to have the authorities look out for him.

Miss Mary **Cox**, of Louisville, received the medal at the Gold Medal contest, at that place last night.

J.T. **Sexton**, of Morganton, desires to say that he joined the church at Mt. Lebanon last Saturday and was baptized in the evening at 3 o'clock p.m. and on Sabbath was liberated to exercise his gift in preaching.

A son of Ad **Gibson** died in the 8th District, Sunday night.

Wednesday, November 20, 1889

Died---On the 9th day of the present month (November) 1889, at the home of her husband near White Pine, Jefferson County, Tennessee, Mrs. H.E. **Carson**, wife of Robert H. Carson who is left with five surviving children to mourn her loss.

One son, Rev. A.N. Carson, D.D., is a graduate of Maryville College, and now has charge of a Presbyterian Church in Piqua, Ohio.

Deceased was born Feb. 11th, 1829, and consequently at the time of her death was within two days of being sixty-three years and nine months old. She was the daughter of the late Thomas **Rankin**, a ruling elder in the Hopewell Presbyterian Church, of Dandridge, Tenn. She was converted in early life, and united with the Presbyterian Church, of which she remained a faithful and exemplary member till the time of her death. She loved the house of God, and with her husband and children, was a regular and devout attendant on its sacred services. Her faithful and loving ministrations at the bedside of the sick will long be remembered in her neighborhood. She possessed an equable temper and a sound Christian judgment, so that "The hearts of her husband and children safely trusted in her, and she did them good and not evil all the days of her life." She lived so as to be missed. She will be missed in the little church of Westminster where her seat will be vacant when the congregation assemble to worship God. She will be missed by her neighbors and numerous friends: But O, how sadly will she be missed at home, where she was the companion and ministering angel to an aged and almost entirely deaf husband. But her labors are over, her warfare is ended, she has "fought a good fight, she has kept the faith," and on that other bright shore she awaits those dear ones who will now miss her so much on earth. ---A former pastor, James **McNeal**.

The First Snow---On Monday evening, a little before daybreak, Maryville experienced the first snow of the season. Owing to the soaked condition of the ground, none of it "stuck." The Chilhowee Mountains are covered with snow.

The house of J.L. **Lane**, a saddler, was burglarized, one day last week. In the absence of his wife, Mr. Lane was boarding at Doc **Hughes**, while Mr. Lane was eating his supper, burglars entered the house, broke open his trunk and secured $23.

My wife, Sarah **Stafford**, having left my bed and board with a suckling child on the 18th of Nov., 1889, I hereby notify all persons not to harbor or keep her about them as she left without any just cause and while I was absent from home. ---William Stafford.

Wednesday, November 27, 1889

Capt. W.H. **Kirk**, an old citizen of this place and an ex-postmaster, died yesterday morning, at 8 o'clock. Mr. Kirk died from a stroke of paralysis. He was at Knoxville Monday, and up in town Monday night, and was taken sick 1 o'clock Tuesday morning, being sick only eight hours.

A Miss **Cooper**, an employee of the Rockford Cotton Mills, died on Sunday. We did not learn any particulars.

Hoeg **Beals** died last week, near Friendsville.

Mrs. William **Goddard**, mother of James and Elias Goddard, died Sunday afternoon at two o'clock. She was buried Monday afternoon at two o'clock.

The wife of William **Brewer**, near Rockford, died last Friday.

William H. **McNeal**, of Long Hollow, for a number of years, Justice of Peace, died on last Wednesday, age 78 years.

Jesse **Stanley**, who has been connected with blacksmithing near the depot, left Thursday morning for Richmond, Ind., to locate near there.

Mrs. Joseph E. **Houston**, a very excellent lady about 78 years, died at Madisonville last week. She has many friends and relatives in this county.

Wednesday, December 4, 1889

Lewis Dead And Buried On Bald Mountain, Near The Toll Gate--- W.M. **Lewis** is a Negro who worked in the chain-gang here for three months. He was regarded while here as a desperate fellow. He even threatened to kill some of the officers. On his release from jail, he went back to the railroad works, on the Knoxville Southern, one mile below Unitia. On last Tuesday, Lewis was wanted as a witness in the case of the State against Wiley **Gaither** and Macy **Mills**. Sheriff **Armstrong**, who was with Deputy **Blankenship** and Constable **Coker**, in charge of these parties, was going to summon Lewis but Blankenship said, "Let me go, I know Lewis better than you do." On arriving at his house and asking his wife where Lewis was, Blankenship was shot by Lewis who was standing at the corner of the house, 100 shot lodged in Deputy Blankenship's thigh. He was conveyed to Mr. **Kaiser**'s where he stayed until he was brought home on Monday. At this time he is resting very well.

Lewis was chased into Loudon County by different parties and there, at **Thompson**'s store the officers with M.H. **Edmondson**, got on his trail. Lewis slept Thursday night at Irwin **Jones**, one mile beyond **Wells**' Mill. The officers on Friday morning were about seven or eight miles behind Lewis. From Jones', Lewis went up the river. Coker's horse failed at Dave **Smith**'s, and he left his horse there, taking one of Smith's. Smith there joined the party. From the people living along the road, they found out Lewis' movement. He carried his gun cocked whenever he passed a house.

From Dave Smith's store to the toll gate it is about 18 miles. They arrived there about 12 o'clock. Lewis was then said to be about 15 minutes ahead of them, one mile and a half from the toll gate. Mr. Edmondson was riding a short distance in front of the rest of the party, when he suddenly saw Lewis with his gun raised, ready to fire. Before he could say or do anything Lewis shot him, the ball striking Mr. Edmondson on the thigh. On the arrival of the officers, Mr. Edmondson told them that he was shot but for them to go on and catch the Negro. On

133

reaching Lewis, they found that he was shot but it is not known who shot him. Mr. Edmondson was carried on an improvised stretcher to the toll gate, where he stayed until a hack could be brought from John **Howard**'s, about 6 miles, when he was taken to Dave Smith's. At 10 o'clock, news reached here of the occurrence, and Perry Edmondson, Dr. Blankenship and a hack left for Smith's, arriving there about 7 o'clock Saturday morning. The hack bringing Mr. Edmondson got in town about six o'clock and he was taken from here, on the train to his home. At last account he was resting comfortable, although the wound is a serious one. Mr. Edmondson stood the trip very well and showed remarkable coolness and bravery. After being shot he sat on his horse until the rest of the party came back from capturing the Negro.

Lewis fought until the last. He was brought down to the toll gate, but after he had been there a short time he became delirious, trying to bite and kick the officers. About 11 Friday night, he died, and was probably buried close to where he died. Lewis showed great fortitude and endurance. He traveled 25 miles on Friday morning, which is a good journey for a horse in that length of time, 8 of the 23 miles were up Bald Mountain. He was a reckless, desperate fellow; always feared by the neighbors where he lived. It is said he had been a penitentiary convict in North Carolina. At the time he was killed he was making his way toward Johnson City, where his wife was to join him. He said he meant to kill Sheriff Armstrong, instead of Edmondson, but if he had not been shot he would have endeavored to kill all of them.

The officers are under great obligations to John Howard for his help. They were in a desperate situation, being on a mountain, no doctor near, 3 inches of snow, their horses had escaped and were in North Carolina and they had to carry Mr. Edmondson to the toll gate, one mile and a half distant.

Wednesday Morning---The bringing of Mr. Blankenship home from Mr. **Kiser**'s somewhat wearied and excited him, but this morning he seems to be some better.

Mr. Edmondson is resting very comfortable this morning. He passed a very good night.

Mr. Harvey **Johnson** has returned to his home in Indiana. He left this country when only five years old. He and Andy **McBath** visited in Knox County last week.

George **Feezell**, of the 8th District, died yesterday evening at one o'clock.

Uncle Jerry **Hudson** is very sick with pneumonia fever.

Wednesday, December 11, 1889

A Fight---Another fight caused by liquor. This is what the *Times* reporter heard on inquiring what caused the excitement on the streets last Thursday afternoon. Will **Barger** had been taking care of a drunken man, and was drinking himself. John **Walker** told someone that anyone that would take care of that man was a s---. Barger went up to Walker and asked him if he said the above. John did not answer but tried to strike Bill but was checked by a blow from Bill's fist, which landed on John's nose. After this, John ran into **Greer**'s meat shop and grabbed the cleaver but this was taken away from him before he could do any hurt. The affair finally ended up in Barger stabbing Walker in the back, and cutting his mouth and tongue. Walker was taken to Dr. **Hannum**'s office and his wounds sewed up. On Thursday night he was unable to speak.

Warrants were sworn out by Louis **Kennedy** for the above parties and a trial set for 6 o'clock, Friday evening, before 'Squire Hannum. John Walker was unable to appear and Barger was turned loose on the plea of self defense.

William **Henry** Fatally Hurt---News reached the city, Sunday evening of a very unfortunate occurrence in the 14th District. About dark, Buck **Frye** went to the house where John and Will Henry live. He was talking to John about the cutting of his cow's tail. Will was returning from watering the stock when he heard Buck accuse him of cutting his (Frye's) cow's tail. Will told him that anyone who said that was a liar. It seems that Frye had brought his boy along who had a pair of hames. On Henry saying the above, Frye picked up the hames and struck Will Henry on the head, breaking his skull so that his brains oozed out. After striking Henry, Frye went to see how bad his cow was hurt, after which he skipped out for North Carolina. About 1 o'clock Monday morning, Sheriff **Armstrong** and Constable **Coker** left here in pursuit of him.

Will Henry is about 18 years old. He attended Maryville College last year. From what we hear, Henry was not guilty of what Frye charged him.

The latest report from Henry that we have received says he is still alive, but cannot recover.

A Thanksgiving Long To Be Remembered---I did not know when I set Thursday, November 28th to move, that it was Thanksgiving Day and when I was told, I said I could thank the Lord that I had a place to go to, but it turned out that I am thankful for more than having a place to go. I can thank my numerous friends for flocking in to assist us, not so much the amount of labor but the spirit that prompted the true genuine friendship and good will. I was born in the 14th Civil District, raised there and with exception of a few years during the Civil War, have lived all my life there. I have had many things to be thankful for but now that went so deep as the (with me) greatest of thanksgiving. When they had landed us in our new home, I wanted to thank them but when I opened my mouth a great big thank stopped in my throat and choked all utterance. As long as I live I shall not forget the Thanksgiving Day of Thursday, November 28th, 1889. ---Josiah **Gamble**.

Officers **Armstrong** and **Coker** returned yesterday morning from Tuckaleechee Cove and report that [Buck] **Frye** first went to some relatives above Knoxville, and then probably left for North Carolina. They are confident of capturing him.

Wednesday, December 18, 1889

The children and friends of Mrs. Sarah **Ellis**, who is now 95 years old, gave her a pleasant visit, in which nice and valuable presents were given her.

Will **Henry**, who was reported last week as fatally hurt, is now better and has some prospects for recovery.

Mrs. Mark **Simpson**, who has long been sick with consumption, died at her home two miles and a half north of town on last Monday morning.

Elizabeth **Hall**, of the 8th District, died on the 12th inst. Heart disease was the trouble.

Wednesday, December 25, 1889

Letter written by R.L. **Phelps** from Huntsville, Alabama.

Mr. Will **Irwin**, and Cordie **Wilson** were married last Wednesday evening at Dr. **Stanley**'s by the Rev. D.S. **Hodsden**. After the marriage ceremony, the happy couple and a company of invited guests went to the home of Mr. Irwin, where refreshments were served and a number of nice presents received. The company spent the evening in social games. The *Times* wishes Mr. & Mrs. Irwin the pleasure of a good, long life.

Died---Monday evening, Dec. 23, 1889, Lucile, infant daughter of Mr. & Mrs. John T. **Anderson**.

John D. **Headrick** fell from a horse near **Gamble**'s Store, and broke his jaw.

Wednesday, January 15, 1890

Mr. William C. **Ferguson**, a citizen of the Cloyd's Creek vicinity in antebellum days, has been on a visit to the home of his nativity and left for his Iowa home the past week. His father, Col. A. Ferguson at the advanced age of 84 is hale and hearty and was for a number of years a Justice of the Peace of our county.

A large chicken hawk was killed last Friday by Samuel **Levering**, south of town. It measured four feet, four inches, from tip of one wing to the other. In examining the inside of its craw, nothing was found there but a big spider. The hawk was killed with a club.

John H. **Martin** of Douglass County, Mo., who has been visiting friends here returned home on last Monday.

Mrs. Rachel **Irwin**, of Niles Ferry, is very sick with malarial and pneumonia fever. She is the step-mother of Mr. Cell Irwin.

Wanted---Cash paid for U.S. Confederate stamps and old U.S. stamps which were issued before 1870, except the three cent (rose color) with George Washington's head. Apply to: Miss Dora **Harvey**, High Street.

Mrs. Eliza **Henry**, of Brick Mill, was taken to the asylum at Nashville on last Saturday morning by Sheriff **Armstrong** and John **Blankenship**.

A wedding occurred here last Wednesday, which was of some note on account of the standing of the parties. Mr. John **Logan** and Miss Phebe **Malcom**. The marriage ceremony took place at Mr. Frank **Walker**'s and was pronounced by Rev. D. **McDonald**, assisted by Rev. J.E. **McConnell**. Presents were given to the newly married couple by Mrs. Frank Walker, Mrs. R.N. **Hood**, Mrs. G.B. **Ross**, Miss Lida **Hook**, Mrs. H. **McBath**, Mrs. & Miss Maggie **Henry**, Miss **Carson**, Mr. J.E. and J.H. Malcom, and the Misses **Broyles**.

137

Wednesday, January 22, 1890

In Memoriam---Miss Minnie M., the oldest daughter of the late W.C. **Anderson** of Rockford, departed this life December 29th, 1889 of consumption, after a lingering illness in the nineteenth year of her age. On the day following her mortal remains accompanied by a large number of relatives and friends, were conveyed to Maryville and laid away in Magnolia Cemetery, to await the resurrection of the just.

In the morning of life, surrounded with almost every temporal blessing calculated to make this life happy, she had much to live for and many things to make long life desirable. But "He that holdeth our lives in his hand," had decreed otherwise, and her spirit so gentle and so kind has returned to Him who gave it; gone to dwell in the Kingdom and Paradise of God.

She bore her illness and suffering with great patience and fortitude and was never heard to murmur or complain.

Few had such an amiable disposition. She would always deny herself of any pleasure to enhance the enjoyment of her friends. Her modest and unassuming manners, her unfeigned friendship, her unvarying kindness and her gentle and affectionate disposition, made her many friends and endeared her to all who were brought in contact with her.

For two and one-half years previous to her illness she had been a student of Maryville College where she enjoyed the confidence and esteem of the entire faculty and made many dear friends.

At an early age she professed faith in the Lord Jesus Christ and attached herself to the Presbyterian Church at Rockford, and up to the time of her death lived a zealous Christian life. She met death bravely. She had no fears of the next world. Seldom has such a triumphant death been witnessed. The portals of the future world seemed to be thrown open and she was permitted to look into the world beyond. When told that her time of departure was close, she exclaimed, "I am anxious to go, they are waiting for me!" and calmly feel asleep in the arms of Jesus.

Thus passed away from earth an esteemed friend, a beloved daughter, a kind and affectionate sister. And although she is gone there is much to lessen the grief of her numerous friends and relatives when they consider her pure and spotless life and her triumphant death. For surely if friends thus happily pass away we shall meet them all again in the world beyond the grave, for it is written "I will ransom them from the power of the grave, I will redeem them from death, O, death I will be thy plagues! O, grave I will be thy destruction." In hopes of a glorious resurrection.;

"Peaceful be thy dreamless sleep

Angels o'er thee vigil keep,
Well we know thou live'st again
In the world above where God doth reign."

To the *Maryville Times*: Another serenade on Ellejoy, Mr. **Ransom Garner** brought in his new wife on the 13th of this inst., and was serenaded by his friends, the doors was opened and all made welcome, the cream jar and winding blades was at their proper places and none broken. There was no assault made with chairs and no profane language used and we wish Mr. & Mrs. Garner a long life and a happy one.

G.G. **O'Conner**, of Middlesettlements and Mrs. **Hunt** were married Monday evening by Rev. D.S. **Hodsden**. Mrs. Hunt came over on the train from Knoxville and the ceremony occurred at the depot.

A second trial was given Ben **Taylor**, by the church at Carpenter's. The trial occupied four days last week and the greatest excitement prevails. The committee returned a verdict of guilty and not guilty. Three said guilty of improper conduct but not guilty of adultery; two of the committee said guilty of adultery and the other member of the committee said improper conduct; but the church it is said will take an appeal to the Elder. It is difficult now to tell the effect of this church trouble. The membership are almost a unit in their opinion and feelings and are very much dissatisfied with the verdict, so we learn.

Pistol Creek had a boom Monday night. Ten inches of solid water fell during the night.

Miss Eliza **Bingham**, Yellow Sulphur, was the lucky guesser of the china set at **Thornton**'s. She guessed 4049.

A fire was seen from here, Monday morning, about five o'clock. It proved to be the barn of Thompson **Cox**, three miles below Louisville, 500 bushels of corn, a new clover huller, some hay, etc., burned. John Cox had gone to the barn to feed and the lantern which he carried exploded, setting fire to the barn.

Mr. William **Henry**, the young man who was knocked speechless and his skull fractured by a Mr. [Buck] **Frye**, is now giving promise of recovery. The last account to us said he was able to talk and was in his right mind. The *Times* is pleased to hear of this recovery.

A daughter of James **Fifer**, died last Saturday at her home below Louisville, Tenn.

Mrs. A.P. **Chapman**, of Cloyd's Creek, is visiting her sister, Mrs. Wiley **Adams** in Missouri.

E.L. **Tolbert** and family have removed to Maryville from Phoenix, S.C.. Mr. Tolbert expects to make his home here. The *Times* welcomes him to this fair land and fine climate.

Wednesday, January 29, 1890

James W. **Martin**, of Maryville, was married at 7 o'clock last evening to Miss Maggie E. **McCulloch**, of this city.
The ceremony occurred at the Third Presbyterian Church parsonage, Rev. W.A. **Harrison**, D.D. officiating. The couple will reside in Maryville. ---*Knoxville Journal*. They have decided to make their home in Knoxville.

The verdict of the committee in the Ben C. **Taylor** case at Carpenter's Campground Jan. 18: In the charge of adultery against B.C. Taylor, we the following members of the committee vote on specification first not guilty, on specification second not guilty, and on charge not guilty. Peter **French**, D.W. **Trotter**, William H. **Lawson**.
In the charge of adultery against B.C. Taylor we the undersigned committee file our protest to the above decision. W.B. **Seaton**, W.H. **Keller**.

Hebronville, January 27---Samuel **McNally**'s wife died on the 21st inst.

Letter written by Mary **Clemens** from Wellsville, Utah, January 18, 1890.

The Forest Hill Presbyterian Church building that was burned last April has been rebuilt near the old ground, and is now occupied. Rev. John **Reagan** as stated supply.

Rev. A.C. **Benson** and Miss Mollie **Pope**, of Honey Grove, Texas, were married in the later part of December. Miss Mollie is a daughter of Rev. T.J. Pope, who used to live in this county. And was a member of the Holston Conference of the M.E. Church, South.

We saw $15 of Confederate money sell for twenty-five cents on last Monday. Mr. **Badger** of Massachusetts, bought it, of David **Goddard**. Mr. Badger wished it to show to his boys.

The second Quarterly meeting for the Maryville circuit, M.E. Church, South, will be held on next Saturday and Sunday at Mt. Moriah.

Died---On Monday night, Sam **Edmondson**, son of M.H. Edmondson. Funeral yesterday evening at 3:30. Interred in Magnolia Cemetery.

Mr. H.H. **Heeb** came home on account of the sickness of his wife, who is now convalescent. Mr. Heeb has been very successful in his work in Georgia, in a building and loan associational organizations.

A son of John **Jeffreys**, near Ellejoy, died last Sunday.

Wednesday, February 5, 1890

Gamble's Store---Charlie, son of J.D. **Headrick**, fell from the upper story of the barn last week and alighting across the wagon bed, was dead for awhile, but is out on foot now.

Hebronville, January 30---Edward, son of John **Jeffers**, died on the 26th inst. Charlie, son of John D. **Hedrick**, fell from the barn the 27th inst., and is badly hurt. He was not able to speak late the same evening. ---John M. **Waters**.

Letter written by A. **Kennedy**, age 88.

[Circuit Court Proceedings, names mentioned are: Wash **Johnson**, J. **Welchins**, Mary **Latham**, Steve **Hutsell**, Sallie **Caton**, Eli **Scate**, Mary **Scate**, William **Garner**, J.H. **Blair**, Frank **Adney**, Sarah **Baker**, Charles **Saffell**, John **Rodgers**, Henry **Bell**, Mary **Gregory**, William **Gregory**, Tempy **Carnes**, E.C. **Carnes**, Mary **Bazzell**, Henry **Bazzell**, A.J. **Bishop**, Riley **Freeman**, Ann E. **Golden** and William T. **Golden**.]

Mrs. Ham **Thompson** died at her home in the Ninth District on the 31st ult. [Jan.] Her disease was cancer.

A new post-office has been erected at Tomotly, near Tomotly Ford of the Little Tennessee River. H. **Hammontree** is postmaster, J.R. **Vaden** assistant postmaster.

John **Fuller**, formerly of this county, died at his home at Sale Creek, in Hamilton County, Tenn., on the 22nd of last January.

The sale of G.W. **Feezell** last Saturday was largely attended. The property sold amounted to $181.25. There was a large amount of old property sold.

Miss Etta **Bond**, well known here, is very low with consumption.

Wednesday, February 12, 1890

Letter written by R.L. **Phelps** from Americus, Georgia.

Hebronville, February 11---I learned this morning that Malinda, wife of J.H. **Walker** of Miller's Cove, is very sick and it is thought that she will die. Also, her oldest daughter, Rozetta, was thought to be dying yesterday evening. They both have fever.
The statement in the former issue of the *Times* of Porter **Inman**'s festival is wrong. It was on Charlie **Watkins**' farm. William **Pate** is a well known colored gentleman of Hebronville, of high-toned Christian character and would not submit to such a gathering on his premises. We are informed that it was a regular hoe-down, rail-burning dance. The above statement referred to was located at Gamble's Store.

Soonerville, February 11---Well, Soonerville is a new town, three miles from Montvale Springs on Montvale and Maryville Pike, though the pike has sunk now about two feet under the mud here, but that little affair does not stop the onward march of our town.

Green **Cupp**, an old citizen of the 8th District, died this morning at 2 o'clock of chronic gravel.

A little son of Dick **Everett** had his hand cut off on Monday last.

John **Blankenship** and John **Pruner** took Henry **Bell** to Knoxville, where they turned him over to the penitentiary lessees. Three years for false pretense was hi sentence.

Kathaleen **Hannum**, (col.) daughter of Dave Hannum, died Saturday night of consumption. Her brothers, Scott and Roy, of Knoxville, attended the funeral.

Mr. [C.A.] **McCarn**, of Iowa, has sent his household goods here and he with his family will be here in a short time.

It is said that in 1832 there was a winter here like the present one. And if our recollection is correct, the cholera followed in 1833.

Wednesday, February 19, 1890

Three Ancient Nails---William **Walker**, of Miller's Cove, brought in three nails that were made by hand, one hundred years ago. They were used in building the first church house in Miller's Cove, in Blount County, Tenn. They were made nearer in the shape of a horse shoe nail, only that they are much heavier. As a relic of one hundred years ago to any of the old families of this part of the State of Tennessee they ought certainly to be valuable, not only for the length of time since they were made but their style and manner of make showing what has been accomplished in mechanic arts since that time.

Friendsville, February 18---Mr. George W. **Lane** was married last week to Miss Lena **Wright** of Long Hollow. Henry **McCully**, an old and well known citizen of the 5th District and a veteran of the late war is seriously ill, and is not expected to recover.

Gamble's Store---Miss Rosa **Walker**, daughter of Houston Walker, died at her home in Miller's Cove, on the morning of the 11th inst., and the remains was interred in the old Baptist burying grounds on the day following at 11 o'clock. The bereaved family have the deepest sympathy of their many friends. Mrs. Walker, Rosa's mother, is thought to be a little better.

Big Gulley---John **Wells** has moved three times this fall. He has gone to Monroe County where taxes are low. Zachariah **Jiles** got his leg broke the other day just below the knee. He was standing behind the carriage of the saw-mill as it run back.

Hebronville, February 14---Rev. James R. **Coulter** preached at Bethlehem last Sabbath. He appealed to the church and people to do righteousness, and without a public confession God would return and do them hurt. Sarah Rozetta , daughter of J.H. **Walker**, of Miller's Cove, died on the 11th inst., at 2 o'clock a.m. She died in the full triumph of a

143

living faith. She praised God and sung songs of praise all through her sickness. Her last words were, "I soon will pass over." Her mother was a little better on the 12th inst., and if she does not relapse, will get well.

Mr. C.A. **McCarn**, of Davenport, Iowa, will commence a course of three lectures on Phrenology and Physiognomy at New Providence Church, on Thursday, Feb. 20, at 7:30 p.m. First lecture free. Come everybody.

Mr. [C.A.] **McCarn** and wife, and son and wife arrived here from Iowa last Thursday evening. They have come here for the benefit of Mrs. McCarn's health, she having asthma. They came via Chicago and Cincinnati.

Mrs. Margaret P. **Newby**, the mother of James and William Newby, died at her home with Matthew **Terrell**. Aged eighty-three years. Disease: bronchitis.

David Green **Cupp** was born in the year 1822 and died Feb. 12, 1890. Aged 68 years. He was born, lived and died on the same farm. He united himself with the Evangelical Lutheran Church in the year 1874 in which he lived a consistent and pious member until his death. He was a ruling Elder in St. John's Evangelical Lutheran Church for sixteen years. He was married twice. His last wife died eight years ago. He was the father of ten children, seven of whom live to mourn the irreparable loss of a kind father.

We are sorry to state that Stephen **Post** is threatened with blindness. The sight of one eye is entirely gone.

Mrs. **Costner**, an aged lady of Carpenter's Campground has knit six counterpanes and pieced thirty-eight log-cabin quilts in the last ten years, and is still able to piece more.

Henry Stanley **Newman**, an able minister from England, will preach at the Friends Church next Sabbath. The public are cordially invited.

Mrs. Ross **Anderson** died at her home near Rockford, Tenn. Was interred in Magnolia Cemetery yesterday.

Wednesday, February 26, 1890

144

A Relic Of The Past---Aaron **Sharp**, in cutting and splitting an oak tree into boards near Maryville, found imbedded in the center cut of the tree, a large lead ball, seventeen inches from the outside of the tree. How and when it went into the tree is simply a conjecture. Evidently to us it must have been during the Indian War or else the War of 1861-65, and from the position it would indicate a remoter period than the sixties of this century.

A child of George **Marshall**, who lives close to town, died yesterday.

Sylvester **Law**, an old man of the Fourteenth District, died yesterday of paralysis.

Uncle Jerry **Hudson** has been confined to his bed quite a portion of the time this winter, but his faith in God remains as bright as ever. Uncle Jerry is always glad to see his old friends and acquaintances, therefore do not forget to call on him.

A child of Mr. **Bittle**'s is very low with pneumonia. His other children have the measles. Later--- Mr. Bittle's child died yesterday evening.

Wednesday, March 5, 1890

Clear Spring, March 3---Seeing many reports in your columns concerning Sabbath Schools, I desire to report through your columns the progress of our Sunday School at this place, conducted by Samuel **Hampson**, Superintendent, Amos **Callahan**, Assistant Superintendent. Our teachers are Hiram **Weagley**, Miss Mary Hampson, Miss Mary **Kidd**. We had a good school last year and the prospects are flattering for a good one this year. Mr. Hampson is a strong advocate of the Sunday School cause. He spares no pains in making his school interesting, he quells before no opposition that has a tendency to destroy the influence and good effect that a Sunday School has upon a community. And by his unceasing efforts to build up a Sabbath School it has done good and we hope will have its effect in the future by allaying jars and divisions among the people of this community. ---Milton **Rankin**.

Tang---Mr. William M. **Wear**, of Ark., is visiting relatives in this place. He has been attending school at the Peabody Normal College, Nashville, Tennessee. ---Siddie & Genia **Myers**.

W.A. **Walker**, died last Friday afternoon. Services were held in the

New Providence Church on Sunday, ay 10:30 o'clock. See a more extended notice written by Maj. Will A. **McTeer**.

William Anderson **Walker** was born in Blount County, February 9th, 1823. His first marriage was with Miss Eliza W. **Wright**, by whom was born one daughter, who is now the wife of John M. **Boyd**, of this place. The first wife having died, Mr. Walker married Miss Mary **Sloan**, who now survives him. By this union there were born three daughters and one son. Two of the daughters are at home with their mother, another is the wife of Rev. D.A. **Heron**, residing in Knox County, while the son is in California where he has been for several years.

Mr. Walker was elected Clerk of Circuit Court in 1848 which position he held fourteen years, when he was appointed Clerk and Master of the Chancery Court. He was exceedingly popular and held his popularity for a longer period of time, perhaps, than any person in the history of the county. In politics he was a Democrat, yet he was always overwhelmingly elected in a decidedly strong Whig county.

About the year 1855 he became a member of New Providence Presbyterian Church, and ever afterwards took a deep interest in religious matters. On the re-organization of the church after the war had closed he was chosen as Superintendent of the Sabbath School, which position he held for many years, and there was universal regret on the part of the church and school when he made up his mind to resign.

In 1866 he was elected a ruling Elder, but could not be induced to accept the position. Some years afterward he was again elected and on the 11th day of February, 1872, was ordained. At the church service, prayer meetings and Sabbath School he was always in his place unless hindered by sickness or something that was unavoidable. It was his delight to converse on religious subjects, and faith was his favorite topic. When leading the prayer meeting he generally selected faith in some form as the topic for consideration. He was exceedingly evenly tempered and forgiving, yet very nervous and painfully sensitive. He has often been heard to say that he did not know what malice or revenge was.

He was a very strong Sabbatharian in his views and his practice. While Superintendent of the Sabbath School he almost universally opened the school with the same hymn, two stanzas of which are very expressive of the man and his religious views:

> Holy Sabbath, happy morning,
> Joyfully the bells we hear,
> Sweetly calling, gently calling
> Us to praise and prayer.

Sweetly sounding thro' each street,
And floating on the quiet air,
Comes the dear familiar greeting,
Calling us to prayer.

Basking in the holy radiance
Of this blessed Sabbath morn,
May the blessed angels keep us,
Till another dawn,
And when earth's best purest love-light
Fadeth from our sight away,
May our risen Saviour take us
To his endless day.

On Saturday the 22nd of February, 1890, Mr. Walker was taken sick.
He soon became helpless and grew weaker and weaker until the
afternoon of the 28th he sunk into the arms of death, and his "risen Savior
took him to his endless day."
He has long been a resident of Maryville, was well known in the
county, and his face will be greatly missed.

Brought In---Buck **Frye**, the man who struck Will **Henry** several
months ago, was brought in by Nath. **Sparks** and **Myers**, on last
Wednesday. He was found in Tuckaleechee Cove where he had been for
a few days. Frye says that since he hurt Henry he has been in North
Carolina and Georgia. A preliminary trial was had last Thursday before
Squire **Patterson**, but as Frye could not raise the $1,000 bond he was
remanded to jail until the April term of Circuit Court.
We understand that the $150 reward offered by Gov. **Taylor** cannot be
gotten by Sparks and Myers as the reward specified willful murder. At
the time the reward was offered it was thought Henry would die.
Henry will probably get well, though at any time the wound might
prove fatal.

Miss Angeline **Clowers** fell from the stair-steps at Dr. **Huddleston**'s
house last week and broke an arm.

Pleas **Henry**, of Little River, left yesterday morning for Dallas, Texas,
where he will live with his uncle in the future.

Mrs. Ann **Cowan**, wife of Constable S.A. Cowan, died Monday
afternoon at her mother's, Mrs. **Currier**. Consumption was her trouble.

Mrs. Sarah A. **Allen**, widow of Robert J. Allen, has been granted a pension.

Dave **Russel** was captured Sunday, by Sheriff **Armstrong**. Last August he struck an old man named **Anthony**, in Knox County, and has been hiding since in this county. The sheriff took him over to Knoxville to be tried before Squire **Maples**.

The report comes that Mr. **Clute**, who used to live here, was thrown from a horse, at South Pittsburg, [TN] and seriously hurt, probably fatally.

David **Keagley** left last week to try his fortune in Texas.

A man, who was literally in rags, brought a rooster in town the other day and sold him for fifteen cents. With one five cents he bought some tobacco, another five cents went for an orange and the remaining nickel was spent for candy. On being asked where he lived he said "he lived in Knoxville, not at Knoxville neither, dgzackly, but at Lyon's View."

Cold Weather---The cold wave which swept over nearly the entire southern states gave us a visit also. For the season of the year it was beyond anything experienced here. The mercury stood twenty degrees above zero. Ice from Saturday evening till Monday morning two inches thick. The bloom and advanced fruit buds have been without doubt, killed or badly damaged and the forward wheat plants. Altogether it was an unwelcome visitor.

Wednesday, March 12, 1890

Gamble's Store---We are sorry to lose Pleasant **Henry** from our midst. He is a good boy and one loved by all who knew him. We hope he may enjoy life with his uncle in Texas where he has gone, and remember the advice of his good and kind mother who has passed away.

News Among The Colored People---The many friends of Prior **Sharp** and wife will be sorry to hear of the death of their youngest child.

Columbus **Best**, Charlie Best, Peter **Razor** and wife, Dorcia **Giles**, Albert **Scott** and Luther **Maxwell** started to Washington State yesterday morning, to try their fortunes in the far west. May success attend them.

148

Hebronville, February 28---Miss Jane, daughter of Lizzie **Peery** of Ellejoy is very sick with typhoid fever. It is thought that she will die. W.M. **Wear**, of Arkansas, and William **Scott** of Tuckaleechee passed Sunday night pleasantly with us. Mr. Wear is a son of Lieutenant L. Wear, formerly of this county. He is a fine scholar and is now attending the Peabody Normal College at Nashville, Tenn. ---John M. **Waters**.

Will **Wilson** and Tom **Bingham** started on yesterday morning for Texas, where they will reside.

A letter from Fred **Clute** to W. C. **Chumlea**, states that old Mr. Clute is better and is now on the road to recovery. His many friends here will be glad to know that he is better.

Mr. **Ely**, who recently removed here from Kansas, has been sick.

General R.N. **Hood** came over on a special last Thursday for the purpose of removing the remains of his children from the cemetery here to Knoxville.

W.M. **Hatcher**, of Gamble's Store has removed his family to Knoxville.

Uncle Jerry **Hudson** died on Friday morning, at eight o'clock. This ended the career of one of the most devoted Christians in the county. He was happy and rejoicing until the very hour of his death and was buried on Methodist Hill, where the remains of his wife lie.

Wednesday, March 19, 1890

Letter written by R.L. **Phelps** from Andersonville, Georgia.

Blount County shipped 5,900 head of fat hogs this past season to Knoxville. We would like to hear what other East Tennessee county beats our shipment.

Union Grove---Henry **McCully**, an aged citizen, is dead.

Clover Hill---Mr. Jack **Ratledge** Jr. met with a very serious accident last week. He went a hunting, and the gun he carried had two loads in it. Jack not knowing this put in another load and shot off the gun. The gun busted, and burnt his face real bad with the powder, until you can scarcely tell what color he is. He was at Mr. **Taylor**'s store, Saturday, when Mr. Taylor put some oil in the stove, and Jack went to close the door, when it flashed up in his face, burnt his hair and face, and set his clothes on fire.

Eusebia---Mr. R.H. **Pickens** and Miss Mellie **Hayes**, were married Wednesday morning, the 12th inst., at Knoxville, Tenn., by Rev. **Tittsworth**. Thomas and Samuel Pickens accompanied the groom to Knoxville. After the ceremony was performed, the happy couple went to the home of the groom, where awaited them a grand reception, which was the occasion of a fine repast, as also a number of costly and beautiful presents. The bachelor's club will miss Mr. Pickens. --- Joe **Hooker**.

R.T. **McConnell**, of Cullen, Iowa, came in on Saturday evening's train, to visit Frank **Walker**'s and other friends here.

The bell on New Providence Church has been removed from the belfry, because it was regarded as unsafe to keep it there.

Wednesday, March 26, 1890

Sultana Survivors---The survivors of the Sultana disaster will hold their anniversary meeting at Eagleton's School House, near Maryville, on the 27th of April. The anniversary will be celebrated this year, religiously. Sermons will be preached by Rev. P.M. **Bartlett**, D.D., Rev. James A. **Ruble** and Rev. Caleb **Rule**. Everybody is invited to be present. ---S.A. **Cowan**, Vice President for Blount County.

Friendsville, March 25---Mrs. Sallie **Lane**, the aged wife of Wesley Lane, died Saturday, after a short illness from paralysis. An infant son of Riley **Humphreys**, who removed recently to Knoxville, died Saturday and was buried at Cloyd's Creek yesterday. Mrs. Phoebe **Griffitts** is at Greeneville, S.C., on a visit to her sister, Mrs. **Means**, who is very sick. ---J.O. **Lee**.

Greenvine, Texas, Feb. 19, 1890. Postmaster at Maryville, Tenn.: If there is a newspaper published in Maryville will you do me the favor to ask the proprietor of said newspaper to send me a specimen copy of same. My wife wants to subscribe for it. She and I are both natives of Blount County. I was born on Little River and my wife, then Loucinda Ann **Wear**, was born on Pistol Creek about two and a half miles from Maryville. Her father's name was James Wear, and lived in a rock house.

I married and came to Washington County, Texas in 1848, and have lived in this county of Washington ever since. We have raised 9 children, 6 girls and 3 boys, all grown and married. We have now 24 grandchildren, making a natural increase of population of 33 since our arrival in the State of Texas. Yours truly, C.G. **Campbell**, P.M.

Gamble's Store---Nannie **Huskey**, wife of Stephen Huskey, died at her home at Waters, Tenn., on Saturday the 15th inst. She was sick about a week, and after giving all around her advice, she fell asleep in the arms of the Saviour.

Miss Belle **McIlvaine**, of Topeka, Kansas, who has been here on a visit to her old home, left yesterday morning for Topeka, via Nashville and St. Louis.

Mr. M.L. **Best** of La Conner, Washington, left for his far off home yesterday morning via L. & N. and the Monon route through Louisville and Chicago.

Wednesday, April 2, 1890

Article concerning a bad storm system that crossed Illinois, Indiana and Kentucky in which a Mr. **Eddington** [formerly of Blount Co. TN] was killed.

Gamble's Store---Melvin **Seaton**, of Notime, has been very unlucky, as he was building a new house and got the frame up the wind blew it down, so they put it up again and got a part of the siding on and the wind of last Thursday night blew it off its foundation.

Hebronville, March 28---Prospect Baptist Church is finished and is a splendid building. Its size is 48x32x16 feet. Mr. John **Patty**, who built the above named house, is a first-class workman, both for speed and skill, and we recommend him to any who wish work done in this line. ---John M. **Waters**.

Notice---My wife, Rachel L. **Barbra**, having left my bed and board without cause, I hereby notify one and all that I will not be responsible for any of her contracts. This March the 29th, 1890. ---William E. Barbra.

Mrs. Campbell **Gillespie** of the 12th District, died with pneumonia, on

Sunday the 30th of March.

Miss Alice **Fagg**, of the Fourteenth District, died at her home last Thursday night. She died very suddenly with diptheria and measles.

Mr. W.F. **Henderson**, who resided here for a short time, but after an improvement in his health, he took charge of a mission work at Courtland, Ala., where his health began to run down directly after going there. Mr. Henderson died on the 17th of March, and his body was taken to Bloomingdale, Ind., and was buried on the 20th. In his sickness he rejoiced in the thought of his near approach to his Heavenly home.

Pat **Ellis** and Miss J. **Hammer** were married at Friendsville last Sunday evening.

Mary **Boring**, of the Third District, died last Friday morning. Disease: consumption.

Cebe **Sterling** and Miss Rose **Blankenship** were married at Clover Hill, last Sunday.

Mr. Charles **Handly** and Mr. **Shope** in the 17th District, got into trouble over a valise, which had been left with Handly by a Mr. **Grant**. Shope came and demanded it and was refused and some cutting took place. Shope was finally cleaned out.

Rev. D.S. **Hodsden** took a trip into Sevier County last week, to visit his brother-in-law, Abraham **Hicks**, who was dangerously wounded with a knife, in the hands of Will **Crigger**.

E.L. **Tolbert**, of Phoenix, South Carolina, who came here last fall with his family on account of schooling his children, will return to his home at Phoenix. A cyclone passed over his large plantation, tearing to pieces three buildings, one of which was a cotton gin. So he finds it necessary to go back earlier than he expected.

P.M. **Seaton**, of the Fourteenth District was building a new frame house 16x38 feet, two stories high, the siding was on and the rafters up. They heavy wind Thursday night blew the house off its foundation, but did not tear it to pieces. The wind also blew down some fences in the neighborhood.

Article concerning a trip to Montvale Springs by Rev. **Kaull** and M.C. **Howey**.

Wednesday, April 9, 1890

Letter written by J.W. **Ogle** from Garland, Texas.

Gamble's Store, April 7---Mr. A.F. **Waters'** dog, of Waters, was bitten about the 1st of March and went mad on last Saturday.

Mr. Charles **Best** came home from Washington to stay, because his best girl is here.

Mrs. Tillie **VanFossen**, of California, came here last evening to visit her father and mother and other friends.

Messrs. Dan and John **Wells**, of Dandridge, are visiting their mother who is dangerously ill.

Rev. Angus **McDonald**, of Knoxville was over last Sunday on account of the death of Mrs. D. McDonald.

Mrs. Jennie **McDonald**, wife of Rev. D. McDonald, died at her home near this place on Saturday evening the 5th inst. Mrs. McDonald has been sick for a long while, but a short time before her death, she was taken with the grippe which closed her life very suddenly. She was interred in Magnolia Cemetery. Sermon by Prof. **Crawford**, assisted by Rev. **Lord**.

Wednesday, April 16, 1890

Mrs. Nerva **Cooper**, wife of John Cooper, of Cades Cove, died last week, of fever.

Carrie B. **Aaron**---Some of our townsmen may remember Eugene M. Aaron, and his inclination to scientific pursuits. We learn from a paragraph in a late Philadelphia paper, that his wife, Carrie B. [**Collins**] Aaron has lately obtained the first prize of one hundred and fifty dollars, offered by Robert H. **Lamborn**, of New York City, for the best essay on the extermination of mosquitoes, especially by dragon flies. The judges were Professor **Newberry**, of Columbia College and Dr. Henry C. **McCoak**, of Philadelphia. The prize was well earned, as very close and careful watching and rearing of the larvae of both species of insects was necessary. It was fully ascertained in the course of investigation, that dragon flies do not prey upon the mosquitoes.

Mrs. Hoyle, the mother of George **Hoyle**, of Knoxville, was taken through here last Saturday, to her final resting place in this county.

C.J. **Hayes** attended the funeral of his mother, at Knoxville, last week.

Buck **Frye** is bound over on a second bond of $1,000, for an assault on John **Henry**.

Annie **Kirby**, daughter of Henry Kirby of the 11th District, died Sunday morning of scrofula.

Miss Cora **Fulton**, died at her home in this city, on the 11th inst., of consumption, at the age of twenty-three years, two months and twenty-three days. Miss Cora is the last of a family of four children of Mr. & Mrs. Aaron Fulton, of York, New York, who came here about twelve years ago. Miss Cora was a member of the M.E. Church, an active member of the Women's Foreign Missionary Society, as also a teacher in the M.E. Sunday School. She was faithful and devoted in these positions up to the time of her sickness, some six months since. In the discharge of her various duties and obligations she commanded the respect of all who knew her. She died in the triumphs of a living faith---passing away with joy, could say in the language of St. Paul, "To die is gain." In parting with her mother she said, "It will not be long till we meet." The friends present of whom she took a loving farewell, were Mrs. A. K. **Harper**, Mrs. Captain **Rowan**, Mrs. Ann H. **Neff**, Miss Julia **Lowry**, Maggie **Rowan** and Miss Della **Goddard**. The funeral services were held at the M.E. Church and were conducted by the Pastor, Rev. **Kaull**, assisted by Prof. **Crawford** and Rev. D.S. **Hodsden**. There was no regular sermon, the services consisted of songs, talks and reading the scriptures; and was very impressive. The house was crowded. A farewell leave was taken of the body, at the close of the church exercises. The corpse looked very natural, like she was enjoying a sweet, natural sleep.

Died---On Saturday the 12th, J.O. **Wray**, of this city. Mr. Wray was an old citizen, aged about 60 years, has for a number of years been in poor health. He has been a special object of the good offices of the Masonic fraternity, and was laid away to rest under their supervision in Clark's graveyard four miles north of town.

154

Lookout for mad dogs. J.W. **Harmon**, three miles east of here killed his dog on account of his being mad. Watch your dogs.

Mrs. Joice **Matthews** who resides with W.L. **McGinley**, is very sick, but little hope is entertained for her recovery.

Mrs. W.C. **Newby** has been confined to her bed with spinal trouble and the loss of her voice for about two months.

Wednesday, April 23, 1890

Friendsville---Dr. Ross **Lane** died Friday last at the home of his son, Samuel Lane in Loudon County, aged about seventy years. He has been a practicing physician in this and surrounding communities for forty years and was respected by all who knew him. His remains were interred in Hickory Valley burying ground.

Cards are out announcing the marriage of J.W. **Gothard** to Miss Cordie **Lee** on May 7th at Friends Church at 11 o'clock a.m.

Gamble's Store, April 21---Some few months ago Messrs. S.A. **Patton** and John **Brown**, while quail and duck hunting along Ellejoy Creek, on **Davis** bros., farm, discovered a fine yellow sulphur spring. We visited the spring some few days since and think it splendid water. The spring needs some work done on it before it will be in condition for use.

Big Gully---Several deaths in our community, in the last two or three weeks; Mrs. **Cook** died of consumption and also Mrs. **Williamson**.

Down in the First District, on the land now owned by James **Everett**, a boy was plowing in the field, when the earth gave way under the horse and he fell into a cavern about twelve feet deep and was wedged in between two ledges of stone. The neighbors assisted in lifting the horse out. He was so bruised up that he died in a few minutes after being taken out. Mr. **Pollard**, a colored man, owned the horse. Below the surface there was a rapid stream of water.

Julius **Miller** has removed to Bristol, his mother and family went a week or so since. Mr. Miller left with his goods and stock last Saturday morning. The *Times* wishes them success in their new home.

Misses Florence **Griffen** and Alice **Coning**, returned home last Thursday from a canvassing tour, in Middle, West Tennessee and

Northern Mississippi and Alabama, and they unhesitatingly say they found but two places that they liked as well as Maryville, one is Clarksville and the other Jackson, Tenn.

Mr. [E.L.] **Tolbert** and family returned to their home in South Carolina. They left Monday morning. He intended to have gone about two weeks sooner, but the measles struck his family, and they had to stay over.

Wednesday, April 30, 1890

Hebronville, April 25---Some dogs concluded that they would refresh themselves on some fresh mutton and fell upon Arnold **Davis'** flock of sheep; the shepherd being at his post succeeded in killing two of the dogs a few days ago. ---J.M. **Waters**.

Clover Hill---We understand that George **Crisp** was plowing and got struck with a plow handle and is in a dangerous condition.

Blood And Vengeance---Charles **White**, of Monroe County, passed through here Monday night with his eleven months old child, fleeing from an enraged wife and her father's family. Mr. White and Miss **Cook** were married about two years since at the home of her father in Monroe County. To them was born one child, less than a year since. About three months ago they separated, but we know nothing of the causes for this separation. Mr. White and a stranger whose name we do not know went to the home of J.M. Cook, armed and while there fired several shots at Mrs. White and probably her mother, inflicting a wound on the hand of Mrs. White. White took the child and left. Mr. Cook not being at home, the men must have received pretty strong resistance from the wife and her mother, to have given any room at all for a resort to arms by men to two women. White came to Maryville, hired a rig to drive him near Knoxville. Mr. Cook came here Tuesday morning in pursuit of White. He offers fifty dollars reward for the capture of White and the child. Cook gives evidence of being a determined man. It is said by our informant that White has been regarded as a peaceable, hard working man, without bad habits, and also that the Cook family is very respectable family. Altogether it seems to be a sad case, one that is difficult to see the results.

Friendsville---Pat **Ellis** had the misfortune to meet with a painful accident last week. He was riding on a wagon holding a cross-cut saw when it got caught in the wheel and lacerated his hand considerably.

Article written by P.M. **Bartlett** concerning the Sultana Survivors Reunion at Eagleton School House.

Old Mr. **Tallent**, seventy-six years old, living with his son who is the keeper of the County Asylum, died Monday night.

A little child of John **Blair**, of Little River, died Monday night.

Charlie **Jones**, on the Little Tennessee River, had his barn and corn burned. It burned between three and four thousand bushels of corn, wagon, buggy, harness and other farming implements. Cause unknown, but it is thought to be the result of someone smoking.

J.E. **Rhea** has purchased the farm of Andrew **Rose**, deceased, in the Fourteenth District for $501.00.

Mr. Jim **Huffstetler** and Miss Hettie **Willox** were married on last Sunday morning, A.J. **Pate**, Esq., officiated at his own residence. Jim beat the boys by taking a Sunday morning excursion to Clover Hill. The *Times* congratulates.

Moses **Gamble**, a son of Josiah Gamble, met with what nearly proved to be a serious accident. He was sitting on a fence at the meeting at Eagleton's and cut his wrist on a knife in someone's hands, from which he would have bled to death in a few minutes if relief had not been administered at once. The wound was tightly bound and he was sent to town and a physician called to his relief.

A child of Mr. Will **Gamble**, who died at Knoxville, was brought over for interment last Friday.

Mr. J.W. **Thornton** and Miss Belle **Frow**, both of this place, were married on last Thursday evening in the presence of special friends who congratulated them. We extend to the newly married couple our good will and brightest congratulations, for a prosperous journey through life.

Wednesday, May 7, 1890

Letter written by J.W. **Ogle** from Garland, Texas.

Gamble's Store---There will be a dedication of the Pleasant Grove

157

Baptist Church on Sunday, May 18, 1890. Mr. John **Blair** had a child to die last week. There will be a graveyard cleaning up and decoration of friends and relative's graves at the cemetery near John D. **Headrick**'s in a few weeks.

Tang---D.M. **Patty**'s child died on the 21st inst. [April]

Mathew **Wilson**, whom our citizens remember as a teacher in the Friends Normal, has gone to Colorado as a last resort for his health.

J.M. **Cook** returned home last Wednesday. He found the child carried off by Mr. [Charles] **White** and took possession of it and seemed happy; and the baby was happy as it sung as it went along the street riding in front of its grandfather. The child was found among some friends of Mr. White at Shook's Gap in Sevier Co. White was not found.

The span of horses of Mel **Seaton** ran away last Wednesday when going down to Pistol Creek, drawing a wagon slightly loaded with house lumber. When opposite Joseph **Hanna**'s woolen factory the lumber at the front end of the wagon left the bolster and turned a somersault with Mr. Seaton sitting on it throwing him under the wagon, it passing over him and the lumber falling on him. He was badly bruised. Dr. **Cates** was called and dressed his wounds. The horses ran through town to the Presbyterian Church, turning there south to Church St., down that to College St., across Pistol Creek bridge south, doing no harm to the wagon, and up near High St., was stopped.

James **Irwin** died on the evening of the 2nd, of cancer. Rev. **Kaull** officiated at the funeral services. Mr. Irwin suffered long with cancer. Friday morning he called his family to his bedside and took his final leave of them, and died at 11 o'clock a.m. in great pain.

James **Cannon** who killed Alex **Hammontree**, a year ago last September, near John **Norwood**'s farm by striking him with a gun barrel, had his trial in Loudon, and was sentenced to the State Prison for ten years.

Marion **Keeble**, of Miller's Cove, died suddenly last Monday morning. The Masonic brethren of the Lodge in this city pretty largely turned out to assist in laying him in his final resting place.

William **Rogers** of Loudon County, died of palsy, on Monday the 28th.

Mrs. Frank **Willard**, of Virginia, is here during the illness of her father, James **Binford**, who is now very low.

Alex **Williamson** died at his home in the Fist District on Monday night, 28th ult. Disease: fever and kidney trouble.

Mrs. Lizzie **Pickens** and sons, Charlie and Rudie, Mrs. Albert **Scott** and two daughters, Othie and Earle, left for the State of Washington, this morning.

Wednesday, May 14, 1890

A tramp from Virginia was killed while stealing a ride. His name was John **Tipton**. The killing took place in Washington County, by the breaking apart of the train.

Hebronville---Marion **Keeble** who died in Miller's Cove recently, was Postmaster, Justice of the Peace and President of the Farmers and Labors Union of that place. Jacob **Carroll**'s daughter, Nannie, fell off the fence the other day and it is thought she fractured the top bone of her left arm just above the wrist joint.

Brick Mill---W.M. **Taylor** who was paralyzed is dead.

Gamble's Store---Richard **Fan**, of Waters, Tenn., left the cove last Monday for Indiana.

Heavy frosts on the mornings of the 7th and 8th inst. A large amount of damage was done to tender vegetables and small fruits.

Mrs. M.L. **McConnell** and daughter, Mattie, were called to Knoxville Friday morning on account of the death of a child of Mr. & Mrs. **Ault**, a grandchild of Mrs. McConnell.

A child of Ira **Revell**, of Rockford, died on Monday last.

The Baptist Church at Pleasant Grove will be dedicated next Sunday. Rev. [W.C.] **Grace** of Knoxville will preach the dedicatory sermon.

George **Petty**, Arthur **Costner**, Will **Huffstetler** and George **Hannah** went to Smoky Mountains last Wednesday on a hunting expedition. They did not see any deer or bear but killed a rabbit on top of Bald Mountain and heard tell of some larger game. They saw it snow up there and felt the coldness of the wind.

Prof. W.H. **Spray**, of Cherokee, North Carolina, was visiting friends in this place last week. The professor is still the principal of the Cherokee Indian Schools, and is having fine success. He renewed his old acquaintance at the *Times* office by calling and subscribing.

Sandy **Kelley**, a well known citizen of Knoxville, and who once lived in Maryville, was shot and killed on last Thursday night by Constable **Henderson**, of that city at the house of one Becky **Stevens**, a prominent character of **Gunter**'s flats. Henderson has made a confession, and says he killed Kelley in self defense. A full statement of his confession is given in the Knoxville dailies. Kelley was a member of the Odd Fellows and was buried under their supervision on Saturday evening.

Wednesday, May 21, 1890

Skipped To Maryville---Mr. E.H. **Littleton** and Miss Mabel M. **Jones** came on a flying trip to Maryville last Friday and called on Clerk **Cunningham** for a license to marry. Rev. D. **McDonald**, was summoned to perform the ceremony, which he did to the satisfaction of bride and groom. At least they were so well pleased that they did not return to Knoxville till Sunday evening. We understand that the father and mother of the young lady were opposed to the marriage, because of the age of their daughter, who is sixteen.

Gamble's Store---The dedication at Pleasant Grove was a disappointment on account of Rev. W.C. **Grace** not attending. There was a large crowd of people out at the meeting, and Rev. **Webb** filled the pulpit. The dedication will now take place in August. Among many from town was Prof. J.H.M. **Sherrill**, Samuel Sherrill and others.

Friendsville---As announced the marriage of Mr. [J.W.] **Gothard** to Miss [Cordie] **Lee** took place according to Friends ceremony at the church on the 7th. Mrs. Gothard will remain at the home of her father till her husband completes his medical course. ---J.O. Lee.

A little child of C.W. **Wilson**, died Sunday morning at 11 o'clock, of flux.

The youngest child of James **McKenzie**, died yesterday afternoon. Cause: croup and measles.

Absalom **Jones'** barn was burned on last Sunday evening, loss about $500. No insurance.

Dr. F. **Beals**, a physician of prominence and a member of the Medical Examining Board for Blount and Loudon Counties, died suddenly in Florida.

The wife of Prof. **Rogers**, died on Monday, May 12, 1890, at her home at Sale Creek. The death was sudden, and is said to have been apoplexy, brought on by la grippe.

Tall, oat meadow grass is a new grass introduced here in East Tennessee by a few farmers. The seed come from Virginia. Dr. John **Goddard** has it growing on his lot at his home on Henry Avenue. We invite the farmers to see it before it is cut.

Wednesday, May 28, 1890

Cold-Blooded Murder---An occurrence took place last Wednesday night, that brought grief and tears to many hearts, drove sleep from dozens of persons and aroused the sympathy of our citizens in behalf of the unfortunate.

A cool and deliberate murder was committed about 9 o'clock, of that evening, within one block of the M.E. Church, South, where a protracted meeting was being held. It took place at the home of H.O. **Wilson**. Mr. Wilson a few minutes before nine o'clock, had been talking to some friends at the Jackson House and remarked that he would go over to his room and read some and then go to bed. He had been away probably not over fifteen minutes when four pistol shots were heard in the direction of his house. Two gentlemen rushed over to the house, and saw a man coming out of the house, and in response to an inquiry as to what was the trouble, he replied, "Oh, nothing."

Mr. Wilson was found lying across the bed, insensible, having received three shots---any of which would have proved fatal. Every effort was made to revive him enough so that he might speak, but unsuccessfully. He died in one half hour from the time of shooting.

Mrs. Wilson and niece, Jessie **Ford**, who were visiting at the time in Kentucky, were telegraphed and they arrived here, Friday evening.

Saturday morning, the funeral services were conducted at the M.E. Church, South, by Revs. **Akers** and **Emory**. The body was then removed by the Orders of Masons and Odd Fellows, of which lodges Mr. Wilson was a member, to Magnolia Cemetery. Mr. George **Sharp**, of Lawrenceburg, Ky., and Mr. Ford, brother of Mrs. Wilson, Rev. L.E. **Prentiss**, wife and son, of Knoxville, attended the funeral.

Up to this time no arrest has been made, and we have no knowledge as to who the guilty one or ones may be. Whoever did the killing, followed Mr. Wilson into the house a few minutes after his entering it. Some think that there was a slight struggle during the shooting, as the right hand of the murdered one was powder burned between the thumb and finger, and the skin was broken in the attempt to wrest the revolver from the attacking party. Evidently the first shot had to some extent disabled Mr. Wilson so that he was not a match for the murderer. We hope and feel sure that the matter will be brought to light and the guilty party made known and justice metted out to him.

Since writing the above, Dr. **Hannum** has left the town, and the grand jury found a bill against him for killing H.O. Wilson. A writ was placed in the hands of the officers, and they traced him to a point near Little River in the direction of the mountains. The officers returned home this morning not being able to find him.

Miss Jennie **Peery**, of the Thirteenth District is sick. Trouble: paralysis.

Mrs. Tennessee **Emmert**, of the 15th District, died Sunday morning of flux.

Sam **Coulter** and a man by the name of **Gibson**, had a fight on the train Thursday evening returning from Barnum's Show. Coulter was fined two dollars and the costs.

Rev. B.F. **Knowles**, of Providence, R.I., died a few days since at his home.

Mr. **Barker**, of Warwick County, Ind., is here with his family to locate, if he can get into business that will suit him.

Mr. M.M. **Simpson** and Mrs. Hettie V. **Lambert** were married, Thursday night, Rev. G.S.W. **Crawford** officiating. Mr. G.B. **Ross** provided the large company present with refreshments, at his home. The bride will take her place at the old homestead, three miles north of town.

David **Patty** died at his home in north Maryville, Monday night, from the effect of a cut from a chisel and blood poisoning. About two weeks since while at work in Mr. **Boyd**'s shop, he cut his arm and in two days he was confined to his bed from this cut, blood poison resulted, and from this he died in great suffering on Monday night. He was buried yesterday morning.

Gamble's Store---We are informed that Mr. Richard **Keeble**, of Miller's Cove, son of Esq. Keeble, deceased, who has been out west for some months, came home on last Thursday.

Friendsville---Allen **Haworth** was thrown from his horse and killed, last Sunday. He was on his way to church at Big Spring, and his horse became unmanageable and threw him and became entangled in the bridles of his brother's horse; his brother jumped off to assist him, when in the struggle one of the horses fell upon him, but left life and strength enough to get up and walk about a quarter of a mile, did not complain very much, but only lived about two hours, and died at the home of Mrs. Sallie **Lee**. His age is fifteen years. He was a grandson of Hartsel **Boring**. Jesse **Hammer** has been sick for several years with consumption, he is worse than usual. Francis **Hackney** has been confined to his room for some time, old age and weakness is the trouble. A child of L.F. **Gregg**, died with measles some days ago.

William H. **Johnson**, died at Thomas **Clark**'s, Sunday. Trouble: consumption.

Letter written by S.E. **Smith** from Valdasta, Texas.

Wednesday, June 4, 1890

Dr. **Hannum** Brought Back---In last week's *Times* we announced that Dr. Hannum had left town and the Grand Jury of the Circuit Court had found a bill of indictment against him for killing H.O. **Wilson**.

A warrant was placed in the hands of Sheriff **Armstrong** and he with U.S. Marshall **Freshour**, started for North Carolina. A telegram from here to the sheriff of Graham County reached him in time to arrest the doctor, just as he reached Bryson City. Hon. Thomas N. **Brown** went over to the town as the State lawyer, but a requisition from Governor **Taylor** was not awaited for as the doctor consented to return to his home without such requisition. He was brought around by rail to Knoxville and

Sunday morning's train brought Dr. Hannum to Maryville. As the charge is not a bailable one, he was imprisoned.

We understand that the doctor has made no confession, but on the contrary says that he is innocent of the charge.

The waves set in motion by the circumstances of the arrival of Dr. Hannum did not quiet down during the whole day, not that there were any threats, for we have heard of none; but the curious and excited crowds wanted to investigate the case for themselves.

A blue crane was killed yesterday by Joe **Patterson** that beat anything we ever "seed." 5 feet 1 inch was the extreme between the bill and toe; 5 feet 8 inches the breadth from tips of wings.

The horse of Ben **Cunningham** ran away last Friday morning, demolishing his fine buggy. The horse started at the sound of the train whistle and ran along Depot Street, slamming the buggy up against the College Street bridge.

A Mrs. **Key**, of Miser's Station, died Sunday, aged 76 years.

A child of H.O. **Taylor**, died at Rockford, Sunday. Age one year.

Article containing the Resolutions of Respect for Marion **Keeble** who died May 5, 1890, and Henry O. **Wilson**.

Wednesday, November 12, 1890

While crossing the long trestle of the K.C.G. & L. Railroad near Knoxville, on Sunday, Margaret **Leftwich**, an old colored lady, was struck by the engine of a passing train, thrown from the bridge and instantly killed.

Newt. **Collette**, aged 45, was run over by train 24, Tuesday night of last week, between Afton and Limestone Gap. An overload of bad whisky caused Collette to lay down on the track and go to sleep.

Information has reached this office of a tragedy being enacted in the upper edge of Loudon County, in which a young man by the name of **Goodwin** was shot and killed by another boy by the name of George **Brooks**. They fell out about an old gun. They were about fifteen years old. The Brooks boy is out on bail.

Messrs. [C.T.] **Webb** and [Robert A.] **Tedford** are still receiving bridal presents. Mr. T.C. **Clark** presented them with a green water gourd apiece, last Monday. They can go to house keeping now all right.

Louis **Farr**, of Kansas, who has been visiting his brother-in-law, A.C. **Anderson**, of this place, for the last thirty days, started for his home Saturday morning.

The Sheriff of Blount County received a letter Monday night from the penitentiary warden, stating that James **Hannum** and Will **Easley** had escaped.

Mr. Joseph **Holliday**, of Whitesville, Mo., is visiting friends and relatives in Maryville. Mr. Holliday gave these quarters a pleasant call.

Horse Thief Caught---Last Friday morning a suspicious looking tough rode up to **McKenzie**'s livery stable and proposed to sell a horse for a very low price. This excited the curiosity of the livery men, and they managed to telephone to Knoxville, to the Chief of Police, to know if he knew of such a chap, and he said they wanted him as he had been engaged in some of their gambling dens a few nights before, and had been arrested and fined about fifty dollars, and escaped from the police. So he stole a horse and made his way for Maryville, and on arrival the keen eyes of our officers and livery men seized the chap, and they arrested him. He gave his name as **Werrell**, but some papers were found on him addressed to **Martin**. After he was arrested he bid the officers goodbye, and started, and then the tug of war came, as the officers did not have any weapons, the fastest on foot would be the winner. John **McKenzie** and John **Blankenship** took after him, and had to throw their throttle wide open for about three or four hundred yards, when John Blankenship grabbed him in the collar as he jumped a gulley, and threw him, cutting a gash across his forehead. There, he remarked, "that will make a hell of a sore," and then gave up. So Mr. Blankenship proved to be the winner in the race. The fellow was not gone as long as he thought he would be until he was brought back. Maryville has been treated to several such scrapes, and the thieves have always been taken in out of the wet. Maryville is not a very good place for such fellows, for the vigilance of our officers will not let them escape justice.

J.E. **Martin**, one of the gamblers arrested in John **Arnold**'s resort Tuesday night and who made his escape by walking out of the recorder's court room Wednesday morning, was re-arrested yesterday morning at

Maryville, by Sheriff **Armstrong**, of Blount County.

When captured, Martin had a horse that he had stolen from a lady by the name of **Doyle**, who lives about a mile south of the river, on the Maryville Pike. The prisoner was brought to this city in a hack and turned over to Chief **Atkin**. A charge of stealing the horse was made against him and he was sent to jail by Justice **Leady** to await trial at the next term of the Criminal Court. He made an attempt to get away from Sheriff Armstrong while in Maryville. ---*Knoxville Tribune.*

Lulu, daughter of John and Nancy Jane **Goddard**, died at the home of her parents, Sunday evening. The deceased was nine years old and at the time of her death had been sick about a month. The funeral services were conducted by Rev. **Martin**. The bereaved family have the sympathy of the entire community.

The two-weeks-old child of L.L. **Callaway** on Little Tennessee River, came to its death a few days ago, through mistake of the nurse. The doctor had left some medicine for it and the mother and in giving the child's medicine the nurse gave a dose of what was left for the mother, which caused its death soon afterward.

Frank **Cook**, aged eight years, son of Tom Cook, of Brick Mill, died last night. He run a snag into his foot about twelve days ago, which caused tetanus or lockjaw, and the result was death.

Died---At the residence of his brother, Dr. A.J. **Arbeely**, in Monrovia, [California] Sunday, October 26, 1890, Dr. J.F. Arbeely, late of Atlanta, Ga., at the age of thirty-five years, after a lingering illness. With an abiding faith in God his death was triumphant. ---*Los Angeles Evening Express.*

Uncle John **Thomas**, father of Andy Thomas, died at George's Mill, Tuesday at 12 o'clock. Mr. Thomas was ninety-two years old at the time of his death.

Wednesday, November 19, 1890

Notes of the Colored People---The faith doctor, Mrs. **Clark**, from Kentucky, is in the town this week in company with her husband. She claims to have the power of the Holy Ghost to heal the afflicted. She is a white lady and says that she has been in the work about two years. It seems that she gets a livelihood by selling a few articles she carries in her satchel. She makes no charges for healing the afflicted. While at the residence of Mrs. Sallie **Tool** trying to make some sells, she perceived that Mrs. Tool was afflicted, and proceeded at once to pray and rub the afflicted parts. In the evening of the same day a reporter conversed with Mrs. Tool and she said that it was even true, she was restored. By what means and how long her recovery would last, she could not tell. Mrs. Tool lives close to the A.M.E. Zion Church.

Dr. E.G. **Haley**, an old and respected citizen of Crab Orchard, died last week.

Capt. **Durfey** and family, of Paulding, Ohio, arrived here last Wednesday, and moved into the **Walker** house. We welcome the Capt. to Maryville and hope he will be satisfied in his new home.

T.P. **Cowan** is erecting a nice dwelling near his home, for Mrs. **Blackburn**, who has been in Utah for some years.

John **Morrison** and Sarah **Ward** were united in marriage at the Baptist Church Monday afternoon.

Andrew J. **McCully** of Cades Cove, has been granted an increase in his pension.

The sudden death of Miss Belle **Scott**, daughter of J.E. Scott, at her home five miles west of this place on Monday evening, brings sadness to the hearts of many relatives and friends. Miss Scott was about eighteen years old and apparently in good health when she retired for the night, but later in the evening her parents were called to her bedside only to find her in convulsions, from which she never recovered, death coming to her relief before the physician could reach there.

Parting Words---Mr. James **Hetherington** and wife started for Tennessee, in company with Mrs. [G.S.] **Bishop** and Mrs. [A.] **Goddard**, Tuesday evening. Mr. Hetherington is an old resident of this city, having been identified with her interests almost from the first. He has held several county offices and always to the satisfaction of the people and with honor to himself. He has always had the welfare of this city at heart, and will be much missed by our people. We can only wish him the best of success wherever he may go, but hope he will find it to his advantage to come back and still make this city his home. A number of his friends and Grand Army boys were at the train to bid him goodbye, and these resolutions, offered by Adjt. **Curfman** in behalf of the Post, were unanimously adopted:

Whereas, Comrade James Hetherington by removing from our midst severs his relation as an active member of Indianola Post, No. 154, G.A.R., and also severs his connection as an old and esteemed citizen of this place, be it

Resolved, That we regret the necessity of having to part with our comrade, who, through all the trials and vicissitudes of this Post, has proven a faithful, efficient and consistent member.

That we hereby assure him and his estimable wife that they carry with them the best wishes and sincere hopes of a host of friends for their prosperity in their home in the new south.

That we cheerfully commend them to our comrades and others as worthy of their favors and confidence.---*Indianola* (Nebraska) *Courier*.

Wednesday, December 17, 1890

Hebronville---William **Pate** lost a fine horse the other day by death. Barbara, wife of J.C. **Dunlap** Jr., died last Friday at her home and was buried at the Bethlehem burying ground Saturday. James **Taylor**, of Poor Valley, Sevier County, has exchanged his farm for a farm in North Georgia, and will move to his new home next week.

Rockford---James **Sims**, an aged man of this place, died last Wednesday. We learned this morning that Ollie **Chandler**, who lives about two miles west of here, jumped from a moving passenger train on the Knoxville Southern Railroad, and was badly hurt. We didn't learn the particulars and can't tell how seriously he is injured.

Seaton---I have been reliably informed that gold has been discovered in Miller's Cove, on the lands of W.C. **Lane** and David **Settlemyers**. James **Milsaps** near Melrose came very near getting his dwelling burned last week. Fire fell from the stove flue on the roof and was in a flame before it was discovered.

W.R. **Harvell**, a printer, was run over and killed by a train at Lake Covmorant, Miss., Thursday. His mother resides at Rome, Ga.

J.H. **Reid**, a tinner of Knoxville, skipped by the light of the moon, leaving a wife and three children in a comparatively helpless condition. Another woman had something to do with his departure.

Mrs. Will **Newby**, who has been speechless for the past few months, has again acquired the art of speech.

Calvin, son of Riley **Long**, who has been in Oregon the past few years, returned home last Thursday.

The colored people are making an effort to organize a fire company for the protection of our town, headed by Uncle Hiram **Gay**. Success to them.

W.H. **Heath** and family left for Knoxville Tuesday morning, where they will reside in the future. We are sorry to lose Mr. Heath, and should he ever return to Maryville, we assure him of a hearty welcome.

Take Warning---My wife, Margaret E. **Garner**, has left my bed and board without just cause or excuse and without my consent and I will not be responsible for any debt whatever that she may make or contract with any person, nor will I pay any such debt. This December 13, 1890. --- Ransom Garner.

Wednesday, December 31, 1890

Huffstetler, December 29---Rosa **Kagley** died at her father's home near Mint, on last Thursday night, of typho malaria. She was buried in Campground graveyard. The bereaved family have the sympathy of this vicinity.

Seaton, December 29---Sylvester and John **Law** were visiting home folks during holidays. John is teaching school in the 16th District of Blount County, and Sylvester is working at the carpenter's trade in Knoxville.

The colored people met since our last issue and organized a fore company for the protection of our town and elected Gib **Porter** as captain. The company will be known as the "Sons of Ham." They have elected a good man as leader. The Porter brothers are known to be leaders in times of fire when few others will take the lead.

Died---Reuben **Edmans** died at his home near Waters, this county on Sunday evening, Dec. 28, 1890.

Last Wednesday evening when we were feeling glad and full of joy at the approach of Christmas, one family in our town was filled with sadness. The spirit of Miss Etta **Bond** took its flight into the Great Beyond. The cause of her death was consumption. Her parents have not been living here long, yet she was well known here, as she attended Maryville College for some time prior to their moving to this place. The funeral services were conducted by Rev. Frank E. **Moore**, Friday morning, after which all that was mortal of Miss Bond was carried to the silent city of the dead, Magnolia Cemetery, and laid away to await the summons of the Judge in that day when all will be judged according to the deeds done in the body.

Family Reunion---James **Cupp**, better known as "Big Jim," had a family reunion on Christmas Day. He has eight children and thirty-two grandchildren, all of which are living. They were all present but seven, who were prevented from being present on account of the inclemency of the weather. Mr. Cupp said as hard as it rained that there were fifty at dinner and there was enough victuals left to feed one hundred and fifty more.

Mr. Cupp is now sixty-six years old, and his wife is sixty-eight. How thankful they ought to be to God for health and prosperity. Mr. Cupp volunteered and was mustered into the Union Army in 1862 and served as a faithful soldier until the end of the war. While he was gone his faithful wife labored hard to keep the children in food and clothing. But all these troubles are passed and they are now enjoying a green old age surrounded by all their children. A. **Goddard**, one of ye publishers, was invited, but was sorry that he could not attend.

A Happy Occasion---The most elegant and happy entertainment of the holiday season was given at the residence of Mr. & Mrs. Joshua **French**, Saturday eve, Dec. 27th, in honor of the 21st birthday of their eldest son, Frank. They were assisted in receiving their guests by their accomplished niece, Mattie **Nunn**. In the midst of pleasant games, supper was announced and immediately all else was forgotten. The table was bountifully supplied and beautifully arranged, having a lovely bouquet of flowers in the center. Dishes were served in the most exquisite style.

After supper all repaired to the parlor, where some excellent music was rendered. Marguerite was given as a duet, with Miss Flora **Henry** at the piano and Miss Annie **Davis**, of Knoxville, and Miss Sallie **Cox**, of Louisville, as vocalists.

The guests missed the best part of all, which was the presentation on the following morning of a handsome gold watch in which was beautifully engraved the following inscription: "Frank D. French, from his Father and Mother on his 21st birthday."

Index

172

Index

Index

Index

Index

Index

Index

Index

McCulloch, 84 John 10 Maggie 127 Maggie E. 140
McCullock, John 124
McCullough, John 27
McCully, Andrew J. 167 George 110 Henry 143 149 I.A. 52 Mary 105 William 64
McDonald, Angus 153 D. 18 41 60 69 82 115 137 153 160 Donald 5 33 36 45 Eliza 97 James 59 Jennie 153
McFadden, 95 97
McGaughey, 84 Margaret 91 Sarah 91
McGhee, Ruhamah 66
McGill, Lucinda 40 Robert 40
McGinley, W.D. 6 W.L. 155
McHenry, Edward 19 John 17 John A. 19 Samuel 18 Thomas 18
McIlvaine, Belle 151 J.I. 113
McKenzie, 117 James 161 John 165
McMillan, 39
McMurray, Boyd 81 Joseph 91 Peggy 91
McMurrey, 18
McMurry, 84 Boyd 92 Ellen 92
McNabb, Willie 48
McNally, Samuel 119 140
McNeal, James 132 Rev. 115 William H. 132
McPeters, John 114
McReynolds, Bob 66 Gilford 107 John A. 4
McSwain, George 124
McTeer, 84 90 Commissioner 10 44 45 Dr. 61 Robert 83 W.A. 44 Will A. 82 83 103 109 146
Mead, Fannie 11 Jared 99
Means, 150 William 38
Merritt, Esther 97
Miller, Henry 36 43 John 59 Julius 155
Mills, Macy 133
Millsap, Jesse 129
Milsap, Wallace 117
Milsaps, James 168

Miser, P.P. 89
Montgomery, Col. 66 Floyd 60 Green 14 Ol 67 Rebecca 66
Moore, 84 85 Anna 122 Ellen 12 Esq. 77 Frank E. 170 J.D. 113 Luna A. 115 Squire 38 89
Morrison, John 167
Morton, B.A. 96 Ben 96 Dr. 50 Jacob 61 John 28 John H. 112
Mullendore, Dr. 71
Murr, Jane 110 John 28
Murray, W.M. 49
Murrin, 84
Myers, 147 Elizabeth 71 Genia 145 Henry 96 Siddie 145 William 107
Neely, John 65
Neff, A.J. 10 14 Ann H. 154 Colonel 26 George 2 Nellie 10
Nelson, D.R. 75 W.C. 75
Newberry, Prof. 153
Newby, Anna 128 Margaret P. 144 W.C. 155 Will 169 William 144
Newell, Samuel 91
Newman, Henry Stanley 144 J.G. 113 John 82
Neymond, 84
Nichols, John 27 Josiah 27
Nickerson, 123
Niman, Jacob 64 107
Norton, George 117 118 J.G. 117
Norvall, T. 29
Norwood, John 158 Wesley 81 103
Noyes, Hattie 58
Nuchols, Andrew 19 Bessie 24 James 34 Mary 34 Richard 107 William 71
Nunn, Mattie 170
Nyman, 82
O'Conner, G.G. 139
Odell, M.E. 50
Ogle, J.W. 153 157
Orr, James 104 105
Overman, 130

179

Index

Index

Index

ABOUT THE AUTHOR

The compiler has been interested in genealogy and history since 1982, and since that time has spent countless hours researching his own family history and the history of his community. His search has taken him to many libraries, cemeteries, and court houses in an effort to obtain credible information. In 1994 he served as one of the chairpersons on a committee that compiled the book, *The History of Blount County, Tennessee, and Its People, 1795-1995.* In 1986 he began to index the obituaries located in his hometown newspaper which are included in his 1998 book, *Index of Obituaries and Death Notices from the* Enterprise, *1906-1960.*

www.ingramcontent.com/pod-product-compliance
Lightning Source LLC
Chambersburg PA
CBHW070916270326
41927CB00011B/2597